Knowing the Learner

Paul Zachos, PhD

Association for the Cooperative Advancement of Science & Education
110 Spring Street • Saratoga Springs, NY 12866

William E. J. Doane, PhD

IDA's Science & Technology Policy Institute
1899 Pennsylvania Avenue NW • Suite 520 • Washington, DC 20006

SHIRES PRESS

4869 Main Street

P.O. Box 2200

Manchester Center, VT 05255

www.northshire.com

Knowing the Learner
A new approach to educational information

ISBN: 978-1-60571-364-9

Building Community, One Book at a Time

A family-owned, independent bookstore in
Manchester Ctr., VT, since 1976 and Saratoga Springs, NY, since 2013.
We are committed to excellence in bookselling.
The Northshire Bookstore's mission is to serve as a resource for
information, ideas, and entertainment while honoring the needs
of customers, staff, and community.

Printed in the United States of America

In Memory of Robert M. Pruzek
1940-2016

Acknowledgments

Many thanks to the following:

Our ACASE co-founders Tom Hick, Master of Non-Freudian Regression Analysis, and Cindy Sargent our model for humane teaching

Adriana Gómez Piccolo who carefully and thoughtfully helps us to bring our work into realization

Monica Schurr who in so many ways brought ACASE into the 21st century

The teachers of the *Astrobiology Teachers Academy*, notably Leonard Bacon and Jonathan Heiles and especially Judith Archibold, who learned from the ACASE Assessment Information System who her best students really were

The scientists of the New York Center for Astrobiology at Rensselaer Polytechnic Institute and the University at Albany (Special thanks to John Delano who grasped and had sufficient faith in our vision to apply it successfully with his university level students)

Jason Brechko, master science teacher, faithful friend and colleague and insightful contributor to the content of this book

Deborah Newlen, who grasped the possibilities of this work early on and has labored persistently and faithfully to realize them — she joined wholeheartedly in the process of editing and ended up making substantive contributions to content and expression

The many teachers who tried it out and "got it", most notably Jane Capiello, who pioneered **Cubes and Liquids** and Flannery Denny, who helped make this presentation more readable and relevant to teachers

Master Waldorf educator Gabriele Kuehne

Joette Stefl-Mabry, who played a significant role in the development of our critique of "formative assessment"

Yeshayahu Ben Aharon, who knows how to bring the past and the future into the present

Barbara Glaser, the initiator of the concept of "The 25", our first, and most constant and devoted supporter, who regularly sacrificed her own interests to help us realize our vision

The awesome *Lady of the Red Pen,* who prefers to remain anonymous

And to all the others who guide us toward quality and compassion, including Christie Veitch, Brian A. Danielak, Andrew J. Hurd, and Justin C. Mary

Contents

Readers interested in communicating with the authors or engaging in conversation concerning topics presented in Knowing the Learner can do so by visiting the Forum for Educational Arts and Sciences at *http://EducationalRenewal.org/forum/* and clicking on *Knowing the Learner*

Preface
A Social Chasm in Education

The educational controversies appearing at the juncture of the 20th and 21st centuries suggest the emergence of a widening social chasm.

When we listen to teachers talk about education, the conversation tends to focus on the virtues of various teaching methods, how to motivate students, the joys of teaching. We also hear teachers relate their problems in dealing with supervisors, administrators, local school boards, state regulations, and what they consider the changing (usually worsening) characteristics of students and educational environments.

Meanwhile, news-makers are talking about the decline of student performance on international comparisons and a perceived loss in national competitiveness, about the responsibility of teachers for this decline, and about the virtues of accountability based on educational assessments as a solution to the problem.

That teachers would be inclined to talk shop rather than engage in public policy discourse is to be expected, although always disappointing. But the fact that teachers and news-makers are not even talking about the same topics indicates a widening gap in interests as well as perspectives and understandings. The subjects of testing, assessment, and accountability do emerge in conversations with teachers but primarily as artifacts of oppression and symptoms of the degenerating climate of educational institutions rather than from an inherent interest and involvement in these subjects.

Since the 1990s in the United States, the Federal Government, regardless of the political party in power, has increasingly been intervening in educational affairs. These interventions have worked their way into the classroom itself. The current interventions differ from those of the 1960's and 70's when grand resources were gathered and made available, particularly to address inequities in educational opportunity. Today, increasingly the state, as well as other powerful interests, is directing educators in how they should conduct their business and using test results as an instrument with which to wield control.

The gap between teachers' and the emerging public view of education is such that there is little sign in mainstream education of bringing the two sides into collaboration or even reconciliation. But a bridge can be built across this divide. Foundations of general and common interest exist that have been disregarded. These foundation blocks are at the very core of what makes educational action meaningful. They should actually underlie every educational effort and, yet, are inadequately attended to. Federal reform efforts have staked their current initiatives on the idea of such a foundation but then disregarded it in practice. *Knowing the Learner* is directed toward building this bridge through the re-discovery and application of the needed foundation blocks. The basis for spanning this gap, for seeing through the current controversies will be the theme that underlies every chapter in the book. But deeper problems underlie these controversies as well. Cataclysmic changes are altering the faces of science, technology, society, and Nature herself. Human institutions are failing to realize their stated ideals, failing to adjust to the "newness" of reality. Vast resources are directed to carrying out existing educational programs, giving little attention to the fundamental educational questions of what the human being and human community can become.

It should be no surprise that in this "Age of Information" the hottest controversies are those that swirl around the question of educational information — that is the question of educational assessment and how its results are to be used. But, lying virtually untouched beneath the controversies, is the question of what is and what is not educational information. It is here that the bridge can be built: around answers to the question of educational assessment. Moreover, through refreshed ideas concerning educational assessment and evaluation, many education questions can be seen from a different perspective, a perspective that opens new vistas for envisioning productivity and collaboration in the field of education.

Our book is titled *Knowing the Learner* because that is the true purpose of educational assessment.

Educational and Scientific Discoveries
at the Turning Point of the Century:
A Biographical Introduction

In the last decade of the 20th century, the group of teachers and scientists who would later form the Association for the Cooperative Advancement of Science and Education surveyed the outcomes of our research into scientific inquiry and discovery by high school students. We realized that we had touched a sensitive nerve in the educational organism. What we had discovered in short was that concepts central to success in high school mathematics, science, and technology — concepts that take weeks, months or years to develop in school programs, and which we saw were only poorly developed by the completion of high school — can be attained by students through their own independent investigations into natural phenomena in the space of a few hours or less.

At the point when we made this remarkable discovery (described in our 1990 paper in the *Journal of Science Teaching*), we already had a burgeoning notion of the importance of educational assessment. Inspired by the developmental studies of Bärbel Inhelder and Jean Piaget, we recognized the power of conversations between teachers and students around strategically presented empirical tasks as a way to reveal the underlying thinking processes of learners.

Our findings and methods were warmly received by science teachers. Many expressed the sentiment that the development of capabilities for scientific inquiry and the experience of scientific discovery in the classroom were what had first brought them to teach science. We worked with these teachers to turn our research tools into practical methods for developing higher-order thinking capabilities in existing mathematics, science, and technology programs. But, as much as teachers wished to turn their attention to scientific inquiry and discovery in the classroom and to the scientific study and improvement of their own teaching, we kept running into what we called the February/March effect: "This has all been great, but now I really have to concentrate the rest of the year on preparing my students for The Test."

Recurrent experiences of this sort led us to formulate what we call The Law of Educational Program Transformation: *The information that one uses to evaluate an educational program shapes the curriculum and instruction of that program.*

All who have worked in the field of education immediately recognize this law, its potency and its effects. The law operates in educational programs much as the law of gravity operates in the natural world. It is the force behind the phenomenon of "teaching to the test" — it is the principle that is now being used increasingly by governments to extend control over educational programs and institutions. But we found that within the workings of this iron law there remained a path to redemption — if we can create assessments that truly embody our highest aspirations for our students (and if we use this information strictly for educational purposes), we will have available a resource that can be directed to creating instructional programs of the highest quality, effectiveness, and humanity.

This might have been just another ideal dream of educational theorists were it not that we found the practice exemplified in the *Science Research in the High School* course developed by Robert Pavlica of Byrum Hills School District in New York. Pavlica achieved extraordinary success in helping high school students learn to conduct scientific research in collaboration with mentor scientists. He then extended his methods to professional development and prepared many teachers to achieve successes like his own with their own students. Pavlica's use of what we call *accomplishment-based grading*, served as an organic feature of his award-winning approach to educational reform and renewal.

Our work over the last two decades has been to foster the systematic use of educational assessment findings to support a wide range of purposes at all levels of educational systems. These purposes include planning, evaluation, decision-making, policy development, accountability, professional development, and community building. The approach that has emerged not only supplies pertinent and useful information for all of these purposes, but also offers a remedy to the harmful effects associated with conventional testing and grading. We know now that it is possible to collect information that is useful for educational planning and evaluation — even information to be used for accountability — and to use it in a way that is both humane and more efficient than existing methods. However, to do so we must be prepared to give up long-standing testing and grading practices which serve no useful educational role and which consequently constitute a drain on educational vitality and productivity.

Knowing the Learner is intended for anyone who cares deeply about the future of education. But caring deeply about education implies making the requisite efforts to understand the nature of educational activities and events. It means also, to some extent, putting these understandings and feelings into practice. *Knowing the Learner* is intended to provide foundations upon which the reader can understand what is happening in educational programs today and to imagine how to move to more productive educational environments and practices. If anything can be said to characterize our approach as a whole, it is that many important questions concerning education are best looked at as *empirical* questions. Decision-making in the field of education is carried out not only by teachers, but by their supervisors, by administrators, educational specialists, and, increasingly, by government officials. The basis of these decisions is primarily tradition, convention, and expert judgment. The historic point has been reached, however, when we can no longer rely exclusively on this basis for thinking and action. It is no longer sufficient or productive in the long run. Our habits and beliefs about the best ways to do things need to be examined systematically in the light of experience and evidence. We use the term empirical to refer to this systematic testing of our beliefs and practices based on evidence and experience. Increasingly, we find and trust that our readers will begin to see as well that problems, issues, and questions that are arising in the field of education are best treated *empirically*. Moreover, the time has arrived when teachers themselves must play a more central role in such systematic investigations. The work of answering these questions cannot be left entirely in the hands of academicians, specialists, and decision-makers working at great distances from the scene of teaching and learning.

We will concentrate on U.S. schooling in this presentation, first because we are most familiar with it, but also because, for better or for worse, policies and practices in the U.S. are frequently adopted wholesale by school systems in other countries. Also, we draw most of our examples from science education, the field with which we have had greatest experience. The concepts and principles that we present here are, however, universal and will hold for any educational program or activity.

We have written this book because our educational institutions are failing to make needed progress in building sound educational programs and in the study of education. There are many reasons for this failure, but one is sufficient to undermine all otherwise worthy efforts — our institutions are working with the wrong information and misusing the information that they have.

CHAPTER I
What Is Educational Assessment?

The tests and grades that we have experienced in school are not what they seem to be. Conventional testing and grading exact great costs in time, resources, and human suffering but do not provide their promised benefits. In reality, something quite different is needed to support progress in education, something that we call *educational assessment*.

Chapter I
What Is Educational Assessment?

My way is simple but no one can follow it.

Lao Tzu

What Might Seem to Be Teaching...

A teacher stands before a group of students in a science class. She starts to tell a story that transports everyone back to ancient Athens to meet Plato's famous teacher, Socrates. The story begins as Socrates embarks on a search to answer a question. He undertakes this search because of the unexpected visit of a traveler recently arrived from the sacred site of the Oracle of the god Apollo at Delphi. While there, the traveler hears the Oracle proclaim Socrates of Athens to be the wisest man in the world. The traveler arrives wishing to meet this man. Socrates, a humble potter, is both puzzled and moved by this news. He checks to see if his friends might be playing a trick on him, but they are nowhere to be seen. He is a devout man, so he feels that if this is the word of God then he cannot properly avoid it. He closes his shop and travels the known world, pursuing those with a reputation for wisdom — political and military leaders, crones, teachers of all kinds. Finally, he returns home, feeling there may actually be something to what the god spoke after all, for none of these prominent individuals knew as much as they thought they did. But, more importantly for Socrates, he recognized that, unlike those whom he had met, he knew what he didn't know, and in this he seemed to be uniquely wise.

The teacher and class discuss the implications of this story for science. Science is typically regarded as knowledge that has been established through systematic means. This is correct, but neglects the active, creative frontier of science, which is the exploration of what is not known. There is also a more immediate and practical reason for students to be concerned with what they do not know. This class is about to experience a natural phenomenon — floating and sinking. The teacher wants to use this experience to come to know her students better as learners. She plans to observe how they interact with this phenomenon. She knows that there is tension associated with uncertainty, a tension that she can use to engage her students, but also a tendency for them to disparage themselves and to become discouraged by their lack of knowledge. She wants students to be comfortable, open minded, curious, and disciplined. She informs the students they will be embarking on a scientific exploration during which research tasks will be assigned and that she will be asking for their judgments and reasoning. She will be asking questions and wants them to recognize that "I don't know," may be an appropriate response. Indeed, under certain circumstances, it may be the best response! She ends her introduction by informing

2

them that their performance will be graded, but not in the way with which they are most familiar. They will not be graded on whether their answers are correct or incorrect, on what they know or don't know. Rather they will be graded using three criteria:

1. Is their laboratory report complete?

2. Are their answers expressed as complete sentences when requested?

3. Is their handwriting clearly legible?

So begins an exercise in which students observe the placement of objects (various cubes) in several beakers of liquid. The teacher poses a scientific challenge: "I want you each to figure out how to predict whether the cubes will float or sink when placed in a liquid." As they observe a series of immersions, students make predictions and give reasons for those predictions. They are also asked to describe accurately what they perceive to be the critical features  of these phenomena. Finally, they extend their predictions and reasoning to new situations which they must carry out through thought experiments (experiments conducted purely in the realm of thinking).

...Is Actually Assessment!

This exercise is called **Cubes and Liquids** and it is an *assessment activity*! It was inspired by the work of high school science teacher and ACASE co-founder Cindy Sargent. This assessment activity takes about 30 minutes to administer and is generally perceived as stimulating and enjoyable by students. **Cubes and Liquids** is this teacher's way of assessing how well her students have already attained a set of targeted capabilities. The teacher represents these capabilities in the form of six learning goals:

1. Distinguishing observation from inference

2. Providing technical descriptions

3. Using the concept of density to coordinate mass and volume of solid objects

4. Using the concept of density to coordinate mass and volume of liquids

5. Organizing logical possibilities

6. Reasoning with proportions

Testing and Grading *Are Not* Educational Assessment

A different teacher might have proceeded to assign a grade to each of these students based on their levels of attainment of the **Cubes and Liquids** learning goals. There are six goals, so a student might receive 16 points for correct answers on each of the six learning goals, totaling 96. Four points might be left over (out of a total of 100) for particularly good work or satisfying some other criterion for receiving extra credit. Another teacher might consider some of the learning goals to be more important than others and so come up with a weighted grading scheme: 5, 10, 10, 20, 40, 15 for each of the attained outcomes respectively, totaling 100 for a perfect score. A third might choose to use a letter designation — "A" for all goals attained, "B" for 5 out of 6, "C" for 4/6, "D" for 3/6, and "F" or "failing" for less than 3 correct. In each of these cases, a teacher has assigned students a letter or number to summarize their performance. Students could then be compared based on their relative success in attaining the targeted capabilities. These are typical ways to use assessment results to assign grades to students. Perhaps you have experienced something like this as a teacher or student in an educational setting.

But something important is lost in such grading processes. The three different grading schemes all produce summaries of the students' overall performance, but how well students performed on any individual learning goal has been completely obscured. One student may have missed "reasoning with proportions" entirely and another one missed "providing technical descriptions," yet both could receive the same total score. Unfortunately then for both the teacher and the student, the resulting number or letter cannot be used to plan what steps to take next and to figure out how to improve teaching. To use the assessment results to inform teaching, teachers would need to know how well students had attained each of the learning goals separately.

It is primarily to overcome this masking of critical information that educational assessment will be strictly defined here as *obtaining, analyzing, and presenting information on how well distinct learning goals have been attained*. Information on how well distinct learning goals have been attained can be used to plan, carry out, and evaluate subsequent educational activities. It is truly information that can be used to support teaching and learning. Generally speaking, when performance on distinct learning goals is aggregated to create a single value, critical information on the qualities of attainment is lost.

Scores and grades — in which information concerning student attainment has been aggregated across diverse learning goals — *cannot* be used to support teaching and learning. Grades and aggregated test scores *can* be used to rank and compare students. This is what is typically done with such scores. Then these grades and ranks are used to make a variety of decisions concerning passing and failing, admission to honors classes, or eligibility to play on the football team. Such uses are referred to by the expression *high-stakes* because they affect student lives — both immediately and in the long term. High-stakes testing and grading practices are pervasive in contemporary educational programs, yet they are essentially a non-educational use of assessment results, because they do not directly support teaching and learning. A number of illuminating realizations emerge from this distinction between educational and non-educational practices in schools.

How to make use of assessment information on distinct learning goals is self-evident. When teachers have information about how well students have attained the distinct and specific learning goals that make up their curriculum, those teachers can design appropriate instructional interventions for individuals and groups. It is difficult to imagine any information that is more relevant for supporting purely educational purposes than information on how well students have attained prerequisite or currently targeted learning goals.

On the other hand, it is very difficult to imagine how to make educational use of aggregated test scores and grades. A number or letter representing aggregate performance on a set of items does not give specific information concerning what individuals or groups may have attained or failed to attain in a way that is educationally productive. This problem is compounded for course grades because they may include information on student attendance and other behaviors as well. Educationally supportive decisions cannot be made on the basis of such information; instead what is done is that students are compared to how others performed on the same test. The term *norm* is used to refer to the group against which student performance is compared. Conventional practices of testing and grading consisting of this type of collection and comparison of student information are referred to as high-stakes, norm-referenced testing and grading (HSNR):

> *In general, "high stakes" means that test scores are used to determine punishments (such as sanctions, penalties, funding reductions, negative publicity), accolades (awards, public celebration, positive publicity), advancement (grade promotion or graduation for students), or compensation (salary increases or bonuses for administrators and teachers).*[1]

---

[1] *http://edglossary.org/high-stakes-testing/*

The University of North Carolina at Chapel Hill's School of Education offers the following definition of norm-referenced testing:

An assessment designed to measure and compare individual students' performances or test results to those of an appropriate peer group (that is, a norm group) at the classroom, local, or national level. Students with the best performance on a given assessment receive the highest grades. Norm-referenced assessment is generally used to sort students rather than to measure individual performance against a standard or criterion.[2]

For anyone who has experienced schooling in the United States, it does not take a great deal of reflection to recognize that most of the examinations given in schools, whether they are commercially produced, state-developed, or teacher-made, fall into the category of norm-referenced testing, rather than educational assessment. Moreover, they are designed and used mostly for high-stakes purposes rather than for educational purposes. Grades are, by their very nature, high-stakes — that is, they are designed to have an impact on the present and future life of students. In this respect, their use is not educational. Salman Khan characterizes this problem succinctly and eloquently. [3]

The Problem with Conventional Testing and Grading as Motivators for Learning

The argument is often made that grading and testing are educational because they can be used to motivate learning. The problem is that conventional grading practices are at best uneven in their motivational effects. Some children are motivated by high grades; others become lax. Some are motivated to improve their performance when they receive low grades; others feel defeated and give up. Students motivated by the desire to learn can be distracted from this motivation by grading. Others will rebel against grading and become belligerent. Consequently, scores on tests and grades are not a positive incentive for all students and, in fact, are a neutral or negative incentive for many. To be used effectively as a motivator, scores and grades would have to be used by the teacher consciously and precisely, student by student, with a clear knowledge of what effect the grade as feedback would have on that student. This is clearly not done except in rare cases, nor is it practical.

In general, the effects of grading and testing on the relationship between teacher and student can be detrimental as well as undependable. In his book *Choice Words,* Peter Johnston presents an integration of extensive classroom research that highlights

---

[2] *http://www.learnnc.org/reference/norm-referenced%20assessment*

[3] *http://www.ted.com/talks/sal_khan_let_s_teach_for_mastery_not_test_scores*

the effects on student performance of teacher feedback regarding success or failure (Johnston, 2004). The effects are erratic and often destructive. *Choice Words* is a critical, well-researched foundation for understanding the nature and consequence of feedback on student performance. It also sets the stage for a profound meditation on the effects of praise and blame in educational settings.

Distinguishing Assessment from Grading

Educational assessment (assessment as we have defined it) provides all the information that testing does and more. For the reasons indicated above, conventional test scores and grades cannot provide the information needed to plan and evaluate educational programs, or the information needed to suggest professional development and resource needs, or to implement the currently highly touted strategies known as *backward design* and *formative assessment*. Grades and test scores are not needed to see whether or not students are progressing. This can be done more effectively by looking at how well students are attaining distinct learning goals. In later chapters, it will become clear that high-stakes, norm-referenced tests (and this may come as a surprise to many specialists in the field of education) do not supply the information needed for educational accountability either.

Grades then, as conventionally assigned and applied, cannot serve as a consistent and efficient way to motivate students to carry out the work they need to do in order to take advantage of instruction. But the situation is presently such that nearly all existing educational institutions require teachers to assign grades of some sort. Secondary schools often require grades of students entering from primary schools, and universities expect to see grades to serve as a basis for admitting secondary school students. What can be done in the face of this social, political requirement? Can grades be assigned in a way that is fair and educationally useful? The answer is that they can, if a different approach to grading is taken. The critical change that must occur is to effectively separate grading from assessment. One way to do this is through an approach called *accomplishment-based grading*.

The Redemption of Grading: Accomplishment-Based Grading

At the turn of the 21st century, New York State was the scene of the birth of a successful educational innovation — the *Science Research in the High School* course designed and pioneered by Dr. Robert Pavlica in Byrum Hills, New York. For many years, Pavlica's students and the students of teachers who followed his model earned disproportionately high numbers of Westinghouse and then Intel awards at student science symposiums in New York State and across the United States. The University at Albany obtained a National Science Foundation grant to disseminate the program to over 100 school districts. Participating students receive New York State Regents credit and University at Albany college credit for successful participation in this course.[4]

In this elective course, high school students work under the mentorship of a scientist to design, carry out, analyze, and present original scientific research. Student research topics range over a variety of domains of science, technology, mathematics, and engineering.

Course work consists primarily of:

- Reviewing primary research literature

- Building and testing rigorous scientific hypotheses

- Analyzing data

- Writing scientific papers

- Making scientific presentations

Within their early months of participation in this course, students begin to learn more about their subject area than their teacher knows and, as time progresses, the teacher becomes increasingly *under*-qualified to assess the student's grasp of the scientific content and methodology relevant to the research discipline; this responsibility is left to the scientist-mentor.

Pavlica devised an ingenious approach to grading in this course — one that is transparent, motivating, and fair to all course participants. It challenges the field of education to consider the value of a distinction between accomplishment on the one hand and the attainment of learning goals on the other. Pavlica developed a grading schema that monitors student progress in carrying out course assignments. Students set personal goals for their research in two-week periods (called a cycle). Grading is carried out collaboratively during a biweekly conversation between teacher and student. Questions such as the following are used to review student accomplishments during the previous two-week period:

---

[4] *http://www.albany.edu/scienceresearch/*

During this cycle did the student complete an appropriate amount of bibliographic research?	YES	NO	N/A
During this cycle did the student meet every deadline without additional reminders?	YES	NO	N/A
During this cycle did the student integrate design and experimental efforts with journal literature so as to maintain a state-of-the-art grasp of the discipline?	YES	NO	N/A

Based on these conversations, judgments are made jointly about the adequacy of the accomplishment relating to the student's project goals. These goals are worthy in that their accomplishment contributes to the attainment of targeted learning for the course. They are not learning goals themselves, but tasks that are perceived by the teacher as contributing to the attainment of learning goals. Many of the learning goals in such a course are, of necessity, beyond the teacher's area of expertise, because the student has begun to work at an advanced level with a scientist-mentor.

Pavlica's evaluation criteria are transparent, and the expected levels of accomplishment are designated collaboratively by teacher and student. Performance could be summed to obtain a course grade at the end of each marking period or studied in its disaggregated form to show how consistent performance may have been on any particular criterion. Student participation in the evaluation process is a central feature of this schema. Pavlica never ceased to remind colleagues that his students, for the most part, rated their work more severely than he would have on his own. This course is an example of *accomplishment-based grading;* note that the assessment of learning and the act of grading are *completely independent*. This illustrates the reality of a productive separation of the functions of assessment and grading, and challenges conventional notions of how these two functions should be related.

Typical issues associated with grades surround the question of the "fairness" of their assignment. In the case of an explicit and carefully elaborated process for assigning grades, however, the question of fairness need almost never arise. More properly, the question should be whether every student is empowered to meet worthy expectations with worthy accomplishments. Too often in the current situation, students are graded on the basis of capabilities they attained prior to participation in the course or on the basis of capabilities that they could not possibly attain in the educational setting because they lack the prerequisites. These are the true problems that underlie the issue of fairness.

Accomplishment-based grading can motivate students to become engaged in learning and put forth their best efforts irrespective of their levels of achievement and previous successes or failures in school or particular subjects. Accomplishment-based evaluation of student work can be appropriate for all ages, grades, and personality types. In *An Ethic of Excellence*, Ron Berger describes how this type of evaluation can be made to work even in the earliest grades as a vital component of building learning communities devoted to excellence (Berger, 2003). Accomplishment-based grading can be entirely non-threatening. It is educationally informative and is supportive of instruction.

Recall the description of **Cubes and Liquids** provided above. The teacher's actual wording when administering the assessment was something like: "You will not receive a grade based on what you know or don't know, whether you answer my questions correctly or not. Your work will be evaluated instead, based on three criteria:

1. Did you complete the assignment?

2. Was your handwriting clear enough so that I can read it?

3. When a particular task asks for answers expressed as *sentences*, did you provide responses in the form of complete thoughts?"

Such a grading scheme gives every student the opportunity to make efforts to attain the highest grade possible on the assigned task without interfering with or distracting from the content or process of instruction. Students are put at ease concerning the assessment of their performance on the **Cubes and Liquids** worksheet. They are more likely to share what they truly think, rather than what they believe will earn them a higher grade. Students are told that the assessment is purely for the purpose of finding out what they need to be taught and that there is no penalty for wrong answers. They believe it because it is true! Indeed wrong answers provide precisely the information needed to build the next steps of instruction. There is less posturing (to give the teacher the answer they think she wants) and more attention to exploring the phenomenon at hand.

Once assessment results cease to be the basis for grades, the entire landscape of educational environments transforms. Cooperation and collaboration in the teaching and learning process become practical. Openness, on the part of both teacher and student — rather than concern for personal security or information security — can become the hallmark of educational environments. At present, much grading goes on in dark pools created by the policies of educational institutions and the minds of teachers who must implement those policies. Anyone who has ever given grades to students has felt the moral anxiety associated with questions of objectivity, fairness, life impact, and even the legitimacy of the judgments made. Grading policies built around explicit criteria for worthy accomplishments can be a remedy to this.

Grading schemes built around worthy accomplishments, in which each student has the possibility of attaining the highest grade through effort to create a worthwhile process or product, can become a powerful motivator for achievement and learning.

But what should these worthy accomplishments be? The answer is very simple. The activities designed to result in worthy accomplishments should be activities that are intended to lead to the attainment of targeted learning goals. Indeed, one of the criteria of worthiness of such activities, and against which they may be evaluated, is the extent to which engagement in the activities results in the attainment of targeted learning goals. The reason for giving assignments to students — e.g., homework, projects, papers, class work, or participation in class — is that the teacher believes that completing the assignment will help the student to learn. But what if the student completes all the tasks specified by the teacher but doesn't pass the exam? Who is responsible for the failure? The student? The teacher? The answer to this question is far from simple.

Because the idea of divorcing assessment and grading is so foreign to conventional thinking and so radically different from what almost everyone has experienced in educational institutions, it bears particularly open-minded consideration. The use of assessment results to generate grades is so deeply embedded in conventional school practice that it presents one of the most profound obstacles to bringing about change in educational programs.

We neither advocate nor summarily reject the assignment of grades in educational programs. We are merely demonstrating that in programs that require grading, it is possible to develop explicit, fair procedures for assigning grades that are not educationally destructive; indeed, such procedures could be truly motivating.

Granted, grading necessarily involves aggregation of diverse aspects of student performance and so is already problematic from an information point of view, but the components of grades could well be maintained as discrete items of information, as illustrated in the Pavlica science research course example, if this were needed.

The question of grades is often raised with regard to the information needs of postsecondary institutions and employers. But these institutions are rarely interested in fine-grained information. If what they were interested in were reports on how well students have attained specific concepts, skills, and dispositions, it would be a different matter. Later, we will show that such reports could be easily generated, as could reports of the components of accomplishment-based grades. Generally, however, employers and postsecondary educational institutions are looking for dependable indicators of who will succeed in their respective environments. At the gross level at which such information is maintained — as a conglomerate of attainment, accomplishment, and personal traits — conventional grades tell as much about students' social and economic backgrounds as they do about qualifications for success in particular academic or work environments. By contrast, evidence of having produced and directed a play, devised code to solve a significant problem, or written a political or natural history, all tell a good deal more about a student and that student's likelihood of success in postsecondary endeavors than a conventional grade does. In any case, why should institutions of general education owe primary loyalty to the convenience of employers or postsecondary institutions rather than to the well-being of their students?

Implications

Conventional testing provides results that cannot be used to inform and improve teaching and learning. Conventional evaluation practices exacerbate this problem by making non-educational and often destructive decisions based on those results. Consequently, the field of education as a whole is not making the progress that it could to support the attainment of learning goals, because it is working with the wrong information and using the information improperly.

The examples provided above suggest directions for ways to more effectively realize human potential in educational programs. Courses such as *Science Research in the High School* dissolve artificial boundaries between school and community. They bring together the school community with the community of science. Information is used in a way that fosters community among students, community among educators, and deepens the relationship between teachers and students. Evaluation becomes a tool for community building. Grading is effectively divorced from assessment of learning outcomes.

Struggling against existing systems of testing and grading may seem a Sisyphean exercise — confronting powerful and deeply embedded forces, societal assumptions, strongly entrenched practices, and billion-dollar enterprises. One can easily be discouraged by the apparent magnitude of the challenge. Hope lies in realizing that what is confronted in the features of existing testing practices is not a force of nature. Rather it is a human construction and, indeed, one that does not serve well the culture's needs. It may seem that progress would be too difficult to achieve, yet, at the same time, the current cultural climate is desperate for educational approaches that can outperform the existing ineffective practices and overcome restraints associated with dead and dying institutions. Systems designed to efficiently help learners attain targeted learning goals and achieve worthy accomplishments ultimately will deal with real-world demands more flexibly and appropriately.

Summary

Conventional high-stakes, norm-referenced (HSNR) testing and grading practices, because they are based on scores composed of aggregated outcomes of diverse learning goals, are devoid of the information needed to support meaningful and coherent decisions and actions to improve teaching or other features of educational programs. HSNR testing and grading do not and cannot efficiently carry out any of the jobs for which they are deemed critical or necessary. They do not serve an educational function. In practice, they amount to nothing more than a drain of resources with no useful end product. Indeed, they can only be, and typically are, used as a means for holding individuals or institutions responsible for performance on outcome measures. This attribution of responsibility is then used as a means of exercising control. This ends up corrupting the relationships among all stakeholders in educational endeavors, including students and teachers, parents, educational administrators, and policymakers and decision makers. In later chapters, it will become clear that this attribution of responsibility is itself highly questionable.

Not only is conventional grading educationally uninformative, it can be, and usually is, educationally destructive. Being concerned with the grade that will be received based on assessment results can distract attention from the substance of instruction and thwart the inherent desire to learn. Being concerned with providing responses that will please the teacher in order to assure a high grade corrupts the very relationship between teacher and learner. This leads to a radical conclusion — grades, if they need to exist at all, must be kept completely independent of assessment results. Information on how well learning goals have been attained must not be used as a basis for assigning grades. Nevertheless, the practice of giving grades, in spite of its deleterious history, can be put on a rational and productive footing. This requires methods of assigning grades that are independent of educational assessment. Accomplishment-based grading is proposed to serve this purpose, because it can motivate students to engage in worthy activities that support the attainment of worthy learning goals. The stakes are higher than what is typically addressed by high-stakes, norm-referenced testing and grading. A middle school teacher colleague recently remarked: "Learning should be the high stakes." Grading should never be allowed to take priority over facilitating intended learning.

CHAPTER II
What are the Essential Educational Activities?

There are several features common to all successful educational endeavors. Once these are identified, the intention and quality of an educational program can be made evident. In the closing decades of the 20th century, a lifelong educator, Mauritz Johnson, made a critical discovery, that identifying *intended learning outcomes* or *learning goals* is the key to understanding these basic features and to taking effective action in education. His insights are available to and applicable by anyone who is willing to thoughtfully and open-mindedly examine how educational activities actually work. What emerges is the power to grasp, evaluate, and communicate clearly the essence of any educational endeavor in the light of its intended outcomes.

Chapter II
What Are the Essential Educational Activities?

Curriculum exists wherever instruction occurs. Because they are inseparable in practice, some educators and educationists are unable or unwilling to separate curriculum from instruction conceptually. This causes the kind of confusion in communication that would result if a traveler could not distinguish between his destination and the process of getting there, intrinsically related though they certainly are. Add to this an inability to tell the difference between the process of deciding on a destination and the resulting decision, between the itinerary and the trip itself, and between the conveyance used and the route followed, and both the traveler and anyone who tries to communicate with him are likely to become hopelessly lost.

Mauritz Johnson (Preface, Intentionality in Education, 1977)

The Essence of Education

It is in our very nature as human beings to learn from every experience that comes our way. Learning can come about consciously or unconsciously, and it can be for better or for worse. We may learn to act in the world with greater competence; we may also learn to fear what we need not fear. John Dewey recognized that learning experiences are not necessarily educational but can be "mis-educative" (Dewey, 1938).

Education then must be a particular kind of learning. It must be an intentional effort to bring about learning that has desired qualities.

> *Wholly independent of desire or intent, every experience lives on in further experiences. Hence the central problem of education based upon experience is to select the kind of present experiences that live fruitfully and creatively in subsequent experiences.*
>
> *(Dewey, 1938, pp. 16-17)*

Education then can be characterized as intentional efforts to help learners become better able to meet future experiences productively. But what exactly should these efforts be, and how can we maintain such efforts in a lively and sensitive relationship with this larger goal? Johnson saw that the way to do this was through attention to the *intended learning outcomes* (precisely what we have been referring to thus far as *learning goals*). Intended learning outcomes should be the human capabilities that we value and so make efforts to develop. These could be skills needed to build a boat or write a persuasive essay, habits that promote health and safety, or concepts that lead us to a deeper understanding and appreciation of nature.

Mauritz Johnson was a mathematics teacher, a guidance counselor, a professor of education and, for years, the Dean of the School of Education at Cornell University. In his pre-retirement years at the University at Albany, he turned his attention to what might seem a minor issue:

> *The root of the problem appeared to be definitional: either key terms such as curriculum and instruction were not defined, or they were defined and then not used consistently, or worst of all, they were defined in a way that did not make sense.*

> *(Johnson, 1977, p. iii)*

Johnson showed how these seemingly superficial anomalies create impassable barriers to community and progress in education, how they become the source of misunderstanding and, thus, of conflicts. He set his sights on developing a basis for clear understanding and precise communication in all matters that affect educational decision-making. The history of his effort can be traced from his early essay "Definitions and Models in Curriculum Theory" (Johnson, 1967) to its full expression in his comprehensive book *Intentionality in Education* (Johnson, 1977). Such anomalies in thinking about educational concepts also prevent the field of education from developing the precision needed to produce the kind of cumulative knowledge that characterizes other arts and sciences.

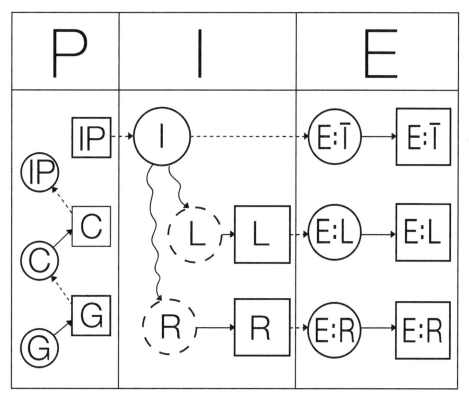

Planning, Implementation and Evaluation functions from Mauritz Johnson's *Intentionality in Education*

In *The Information*, James Gleick highlights an under-appreciated feature of Isaac Newton's contribution to science:

> *...the new discipline of physics could not proceed until Isaac Newton appropriated words that were ancient and vague — force, mass, motion, and even time — and gave them new meanings. Newton made these terms into quantities, suitable for use in mathematical formulas. Until then, motion (for example) had been just as soft and inclusive a term as information. For Aristotelians, motion covered a far-flung family of phenomena: a peach ripening, a stone falling, a child growing, a body decaying. That was too rich. Most varieties of motion had to be tossed out before Newton's laws could apply and the Scientific Revolution could succeed.*
>
> *(Gleick, 2011, p. 7)*

What Newton did for our understanding of *force, matter,* and *motion,* Mauritz Johnson did with regard to the essential elements of educational programs. Johnson's work provides ways to grasp and precisely communicate what is happening (or not happening) in any educational program. This increase of precision in turn provides the basis for building systematic and cumulative knowledge for educational improvement. It might seem that bringing precise definitions to a field of endeavor involving human encounters such as education would create limitations and possibly result in dehumanization or a constriction of creativity. This chapter, indeed, this whole book is devoted to showing that the contrary is the case, that a more precise understanding of what happens in educational processes can make them more transparent and malleable and deepen our relationship to them.

Three Questions That Reveal the Essence of Educational Processes

Johnson recognized that attention given to *intended learning outcomes* (what we call *learning goals*) takes our thinking directly to the heart of educational processes. This insight provided him with the basis for formulating a clarifying distinction between curriculum and instruction and a key to grasping the planning, implementation, and evaluation functions in education. Anyone can access this insight and carry it further by formulating and answering three questions that reveal the basis for understanding and evaluating *any* educational activity. Whatever comes our way as an educational issue, problem, proposal, or activity can become more distinct and, finally, transparent in the light of three questions:

1. What are the learning goals?

2. How well are the learning goals being attained?

3. What are the best ways to help learners attain the learning goals?

Each question refers to an essential educational activity and it turns out, remarkably, that each question can be stated simply in terms of learning goals (intended learning outcomes). Here is the crux of Mauritz Johnson's discovery — a conscious educational process is based on what we intend students to learn. It centers on the human capabilities that students are to attain. Indeed, an educational program can only be justified by showing that it will lead to the attainment of desired learning outcomes. Each of these three questions deserves special attention.

Curriculum — The Answer to Question 1: What Are the Learning Goals?

The concept of learning goals can be used to elucidate the very nature of educational activity. An educational activity may be simply defined as the effort to support the attainment of one or more learning goals. But what can be said concerning an educational activity in which no learning goals are apparent? The absence of conscious learning goals suggests that activities may be proceeding in an unthinking or automatic way and so might easily be misdirected.

The concept of learning goals alone is not sufficient because there are other kinds of goals that characterize educational programs besides learning goals! For example, a student may be given the goal of completing an assignment — to read an essay or complete an online exercise — these are tasks *not* learning goals. The actual learning goals (i.e., the intended learning outcomes) underlying these tasks might be that the student become able to analyze prose structures or become able to correctly interpret the intentions represented by computer source code. Learning goals always refer directly to human capabilities. It is the learning goals that provide justification for assigning specific tasks and for other features of educational programs as well.

Johnson used the term *curriculum* to refer strictly and exclusively to what comes as the answer to the first question: *What are the learning goals?* He defined curriculum as "a structured set of intended learning outcomes." This is a clarifying distinction — the set of learning goals that characterize any educational program is its *curriculum*. Curriculum development is the process by which learning goals are identified. The product, the set of learning goals, is the curriculum. Tasks assigned to help students attain learning goals are something quite distinct from the curriculum. For example, quite different tasks could be assigned to target the attainment of the same learning goal.

Once this foundational role of learning goals is grasped, the underlying nature of any educational program becomes evident and steps forward to greet the observer. For example, if we look at an educational program like Betty Edwards' *Drawing on the Right Side of the Brain* (Edwards, 1989) that develops drawing techniques around five perceptual skills, we see that the following capabilities are targeted learning goals in her curriculum:

1. The perception of edges

2. The perception of spaces

3. The perception of relationships

4. The perception of lights and shadows

5. The perception of the whole or gestalt

Although curriculum is not the central focus of this book, there are certain features of curriculum that critically affect the context in which educational assessment and educational evaluation must operate. These are *the relative importance of the learning goals and their respective domains of learning.*

The Relative Value of Learning Goals

The question of why any particular learning goal should become the object of teaching is the most central question of curriculum development. Because there are an infinite number of potential learning goals, and because education requires judicious allotment of time and of human and financial resources, educational programs need to be organized around the development of capabilities that will have the greatest impact on concurrent and subsequent learning and have the most powerful application when addressing significant human and world problems. Capabilities that have such properties can be called *core capabilities*. The most critical information for educational planning, evaluation, and program improvement is how well core capabilities and the prerequisites to those capabilities are being attained. Information on the attainment of such capabilities can be reasonably thought of as providing vital signs of the quality and success of an educational program, indicators that something that will "live fruitfully and creatively in subsequent experiences" is being attained. In later chapters, it will be made evident that it is just such critical information that is largely missing in the field of education at present.

Whether a targeted capability is a core capability is in the end an empirical question — to what degree does that attainment of the capability contribute to the attainment of other capabilities and desirable effects in the world? This question can be answered only through a systematic study of how the attainment of any given learning outcome leads to various possible desired results. Subsequent chapters will address the need for having an empirical basis for choosing learning goals. We also intend to show how an active role in building such foundations can enhance the competence and professional standing of teachers in the future.

Domains of Learning

Human capabilities and, consequently, learning goals may be categorized in various ways. In the interests of developing the human potential to its fullest, learning goals should address all sides of human nature; the heart and the limbs need to be educated as well as the head. There are multiple domains of learning. Three domains are addressed in *Knowing the Learner* — concepts, skills, and dispositions. Johnson speaks of something similar in the way of *understandings, skills,* and *attitudes* (Johnson, 1977). Valerie Shute and her colleagues speak of "...learners' cognitive (e.g., knowledge and skill acquisition) and non-cognitive (e.g., dispositional and emotional) attributes..." (Shute, Leighton, Jang, & Chu, 2016). Examples drawn from economics education may help to illustrate distinctions between such domains.

Concepts

Concepts are the forms and units into which human knowledge is organized. They are the means by which understanding and knowledge are formed. For example, concepts may be used to identify and distinguish Marxist, Keynesian, and associative economics, as well as to subordinate them to broader categories. These broad concepts can be differentiated more finely to focus on the study of labor, productivity, and exchange — and those concepts differentiated further as needed. From the other side, economics may itself be subsumed under the broader concept of social science. All these concepts may in turn be differentiated from or associated with the concepts that characterize other areas of human knowledge. Such differentiations and associations provide the basis for the richness and diversity of systematic human knowledge.

As early as the 1950s (Bloom, Engelhart, Furst, Hill, & Krathwohl, 1956), many educators tended to trivialize simple knowledge as a learning goal, putting it at the bottom of a hierarchy of cognitive goals below skills such as *analysis, synthesis,* and *evaluation.* But knowledge is anything but simple. In the opening chapter of *What Is Philosophy?* (Deleuze & Guattari, 1994), the authors carry out an extensive examination of the nature, depth, and complexity of the life of concepts. Gilles Deleuze's personal experience of the qualities of concepts on his first encounter with philosophy reveals that they need not be formal and dry: "When I learned that there were such things as concepts, the effect on me was something like the effect of fictional characters on others. They seemed just as alive and lively." (Dosse, 2010, p. 90) Educators will be familiar with *concept mapping*, which is an educational tool that has been used widely for both assessment and instructional purposes (Ruiz-Primo, 2004). Imagine developing an operational concept of "commodity" as a learning goal in the study of economics.

Skills

Skills are human capabilities that grow increasingly refined and strengthened with practice. A teacher of economics might wish students to develop skills such as managing an investment account, comparing the gross domestic products of African nations in the late 20th century, etc. The development of important skills in practical settings has been documented in an extensive body of research summarized in the book *Make It Stick* (Brown, Roediger III, & McDaniel, 2014). The example of a neurosurgeon operating on a wounded hunter in the second chapter of *Make It Stick* illustrates the intimate relationship of concepts and skills. The critical role of thinking skills (particularly logical and mathematical skills) in supporting the acquisition of scientific concepts has been highlighted by Bärbel Inhelder and Jean Piaget (Inhelder & Piaget, 1958) and in our own research (Zachos, Hick, Doane, & Sargent, 2000). Consider *locating and applying primary data sources (e.g., BLS Household Survey, UN Human Development Index)* for life planning as skills to be attained in the study of economics.

Dispositions

The term *dispositions* is used here to refer to a vast field of human capabilities that may be familiar to educators as the *affective domain*. It includes attitudes, values, and habits. Economics has been referred to as the "dismal science" since the time of Thomas Carlyle in the 19th century. This attribution may be blamed on education or perhaps on a failure of education. To its practitioners, economics is a matter of interest and engagement, one that they approach with single-mindedness and passion. All of the human attributes just mentioned (interest, engagement, single-mindedness, devotion, and passion) may be characterized as dispositions. Imagine *devotion to the search for truth in identifying economic influences that underlie political decisions* as a dispositional learning goal in economics.

The *American Association for the Advancement of Science* speaks of "values and attitudes" and includes these under a larger class of learning goals that AAAS refers to as "habits of mind" (American Association for the Advancement of Science (AAAS), 1993). Dispositions should be distinguished from *traits*, a term that refers to inherent characteristics of individuals such as artistic aptitude and extroversion. By contrast, the term *dispositions* refers to educable qualities. But this distinction, though valuable and real, must not be thought of as a hard and fast boundary, e.g., melancholic temperament and introversion may change over time, and some dispositions (single-mindedness) may be difficult to affect. The term *dispositions* encompasses values, beliefs, attitudes, and habits of mind, but also human attributes such as persistence, open-mindedness, eagerness, and engagement. Clearly these can be educable qualities, but the literature on their cultivation and their assessment is just beginning to emerge (Duckworth & Yeager, 2015).

Although dispositional learning goals may be encountered regularly, there is rarely systematic assessment of these goals and program evaluation based on assessment results. Undoubtedly, the composition of this broad collection of human capabilities needs to be differentiated for systematic assessment and instruction to emerge. It may be that the domain of dispositions will turn out to contain sub-domains that will ultimately be as large and important as the domains of concepts and skills to which formal education has historically devoted most of its attention.

At a meeting of the Astrobiology Teachers Academy[5], where the authors were making a presentation on the distinction between concepts, skills, and dispositions, a teacher posed the question — "Which of the three is most fundamental?" The question came as a surprise but fell as a seed into our consciousness. In time, it became clear. Which concepts and skills should be developed in an educational program remains a matter of indifference until we choose to value them for some purpose — and valuing something in the world or in ourselves is a disposition. Johnson made it explicit that in the face of the vast range of what can be learned, attention must be limited to certain capabilities that will be chosen as learning goals. These choices are based on values. The search for values then underlies the entire educational enterprise.

Looking back on the example of **Cubes and Liquids** — the ability to distinguish between what one observes and what one infers requires the attainment of a concept. The ability to productively make such a distinction in one's life and work becomes a matter of developing a skill. To choose to make this capability a persistent feature of one's being is a disposition. Distinguishing observation from inference is as critical to understanding and appreciating literature, history, and the visual arts as it is to developing an operational understanding of density. Consequently, it may rightfully be considered to be a *core capability.* Several teachers at the Waldorf School of the Peninsula in California who were examining the results of **Cubes and Liquids** administered to their ninth grade class remarked that the skill and disposition associated with distinguishing observation from inference would greatly enhance their own understanding of students and improve their interpersonal and professional relationships.

The Curriculum of *Knowing the Learner*

Knowing the Learner is itself organized around the development of 12 capabilities. These capabilities are identified in outline form as learning goals in Appendix A. Each of these capabilities can become the foundation of a significant area of study leading to the development of a scientific approach to educational questions. Many of the citations provided in *Knowing the Learner* are intended to direct readers to deeper investigations of these areas of study. The strategy of *Knowing the Learner* is to explicate a concept associated with each capability and then elicit in readers the disposition to skillfully apply these concepts to educational issues and problems that concern them. We consider these 12 to be *core capabilities*, a necessary foundation for competently approaching questions concerning educational assessment and evaluation and, in fact, all essential educational questions.

---

[5] *http://nai.nasa.gov/education-and-outreach/astrobiology-teachers-academy/*

Assessment — The Means for Answering Question 2: How Well Are the Learning Goals Being Attained?

The term *educational assessment* will be used to refer exclusively to the process of finding out how well distinct (un-aggregated) learning goals have been attained and to the analysis and presentations of that information. As Johnson pointed out, *learning* itself is a quality of the inner nature of the learner and therefore imperceptible. Educational assessment is the means of obtaining evidence that can be used to infer how well intended learning has taken place. We will be using the term *assessment* as an abbreviation for *educational assessment* unless otherwise specified.

Many of our colleagues do not use the term *assessment* in this precise sense. In particular, the term assessment has come to be used in association with activities, like conventional testing and grading, that are, strictly speaking, not educational and can be inimical to education. Our definition does not contradict the ordinary notion of assessment; it does however isolate its information-seeking function with regard to the attainment of distinct learning goals. Such precision has already provided the basis for a productive distinction between educational assessment and conventional testing and grading practices. It will give the reader substantial leverage in productively grasping and addressing additional educational problems as *Knowing the Learner* progresses.

Just as curriculum is the essential *value* function in education, telling us what we perceive to be most important to teach, assessment is the *information* function, revealing how well intended learning outcomes are being attained. Historically, educators have conducted assessments at the completion of an educational program (lesson, unit, course, etc.). In reality, this may be the least valuable point in time to carry out assessments, because by that point instruction has already come to an end and assessment may no longer be useful to help those learners who have not attained the desired learning outcomes. It is most productive to assess the attainment of a learning goal when instruction can still take place so that there is the possibility of finding out for whom instruction is working and for whom it is not. This provides opportunities to creatively restructure and appropriately direct instruction. Indeed, there can be great value in assessing the attainment of learning goals before instruction begins. It may be that some or most or, in some cases, none of the potential learners require instruction with respect to the targeted learning goals.

Instruction — The Answer to Question 3: What Are the Best Ways to Help Learners Attain Learning Goals?

The answer to the third question directs attention to what is typically called *teaching* or *instruction*. Instruction can be thought of as the *artistic* function in education. This is where the genius of teachers most often shows itself. This is what teachers love to do and to share.

Instruction can be simply conceptualized as any effort made, directly in relationship with learners, to help them attain one or more learning goals. Instruction precipitates events in which the teacher, the learner, and the learning goal meet. This meeting is the outward or physically perceptible aspect of what we will call an educational event. Once learning goals have been specified and appropriate methods of assessment made available, there is good reason to consider granting teachers freedom of discretion over instructional methods. The teacher bears ultimate responsibility for the well-being of students and the success of their learning experiences. For that reason alone, teachers need to be able to imagine, realize, evaluate, and improve the activities through which they will bring learner and learning goals together in a particular living context. To have instructional decisions dictated by ideology, by formal rules, by orders from a distant location, by statements of authority, by rules drawn out of past conclusions takes attention away from the reality of the moment in which instruction is taking place. That moment is the teacher's province and responsibility. Preparing and supporting teachers for action at that moment is the great responsibility of all educational institutions and of educational research and development. If we are to realize the full potential of learners, we must first support realization of the full potential of teachers.

Many contemporary educators advocate preceding instruction with a statement of the learning goals. They argue that instruction is most effective when students have the learning goals in mind. This may be the case with mature (e.g., high school and college) students, but might well be a distraction for young learners. The teacher, on the other hand, must always be conscious and intentional concerning the interaction of learning goal and student.

Ultimately, this and many other questions regarding instruction are empirical questions; adequate answers need to be based on systematic experiential study. At this point, the reader may already be starting to intuit that the question and, indeed, any question concerning instruction may have different appropriate answers, depending on the student and the learning goal.

Following from these considerations, we will generally not be advocating particular methods of instruction in Knowing the Learner. Nor will there be much more attention to curriculum (a subject that rightfully would fill volumes) other than to indicate the central role of learning goals and the importance, perhaps the necessity, for curriculum to be directed to core capabilities and to a span of domains of learning. *Knowing the Learner* is primarily about educational assessment and educational evaluation — the gathering and productive application of educational information. There is one more critical issue, however, concerning curriculum and instruction.

Readiness for Education

A central challenge for the teacher is imagining what needs to be presented to students and how to present it. Curriculum provides guiding ideals, but the learner must be prepared to confront the substance of the curriculum productively. There are many considerations regarding this preparedness. One of the most critical has to do with the level of development of the learner. The 20th century brought into general consciousness the notion of stages of human development. Great educational thinkers like John Dewey (Dewey, 1902), Rudolf Steiner (H.Ginsburg, 1982), and Maria Montessori[6], working from different perspectives but mutually on the basis of knowing the learner's level of development, made seminal contributions to this question, identifying levels of development and suggesting particulars of curriculum and instruction appropriate and productive at specific stages of development. What John Dewey prefigured in his critical and prescient essay *The Child and the Curriculum*, (ibid) Piaget and Inhelder would later support through their empirical research (Piaget & Inhelder, 1969). This was the notion that there is a natural progression in the emergence of human capabilities, and that this progression must serve as the foundation for the intersection of curriculum and instruction. Mainstream education is still at a rudimentary stage in grasping the implications of this progression. This highlights another aspect of knowing the learner — that is, knowing when a particular curricular item or instruction method is appropriate for a learner given the learner's level of development. Assessment can help to answer this question and, in fact, may be the most powerful tool for this purpose. But the question must then be posed equally concerning the practice of assessment: Is the method of assessment appropriate to the developmental level of the learner?

The Contexts of Educational Activities

Some additional definitions are needed, as we move forward, to permit distinctions between the venues (institutional and physical settings where educational activities take place), the activities themselves, and the actual events that occur in those settings when intentional efforts are made to facilitate the attainment of learning goals.

Educational Settings — the physical locations in which the learner is found during educational events.

Educational Activities — looked at comprehensively, educational activities include, or should include, the fundamental features of educational processes — curriculum, assessment, instruction, and evaluation. Johnson has shown how such features each have distinct *planning, implementation,* and *evaluation* aspects (Johnson, 1977).

---

[6] *http://ageofmontessori.org/montessori-stages-of-development-for-early-learning/*

Educational Programs — the formal venues for providing educational activities (e.g., institutions such as primary schools and universities, formal courses of study, but also training programs, workshops, MOOCs, etc.).

Educational Events — the interactions in time and space where teacher and learner are engaged in realizing (helping learners attain) learning goals. They are meetings around the theme of realizing one or more learning goals.

Educational events are the special moments when efforts are being made to realize the attainment of learning goals. Why must educational events include learning goals? This is because explicitly or not, consciously or not, educational activities are directed primarily to the attainment of capabilities. Learning goals represent those desired capabilities.

Educational programs exist and provide settings to promote educational events through educational activities. However, educational activities and educational events may exist and be successful without formal programs. Moreover, there are many activities carried out within educational programs that are not educational — the maintenance of health records, systems of eligibility for free lunch, taking attendance, transportation, and all the features of managing and sustaining institutions.

Evaluation — The Educational Activity That Integrates Educational Activities

There is one more feature of educational processes that we present as essential to both intimate educational events and to the larger educational enterprise — evaluation. Inspired by indications given by Michael Scriven[7] and Robert Pruzek[8], we define *educational evaluation concisely as the practice of applying information in order to increase the value of educational activities and programs.* Educational evaluation, in this light, has two aspects:

1. The use of information (especially information from educational assessment) to increase the value of educational activities

2. The use of information (especially information from educational assessment) to build educational community

Again, while this definition of evaluation is not deviant from conventional usage, it is more precise. This precision is directed in part towards resurrecting the concept

---

[7] *http://MichaelScriven.info*

[8] *http://RMPruzek.com*

of evaluation from the stigmas of oppression and dread that accompany the term and to raise the possibility of bringing communal creative imagination to its practice.

Implications

The conceptual tools presented in *Knowing the Learner* are meant to provide new groundwork for approaching almost any purely educational problem. They are presented so that, and in a way that, curriculum, assessment instruction, and evaluation all serve the realities faced at the moment of educational events. Naturally, there are also political and economic conditions that educational programs must reflect. In *Intentionality in Education*, Johnson referred to these external forces impinging upon educational settings and programs as *frame factors*. Frame factors present their own special problems and requirements for solutions. But if we keep in mind that economic and political forces should never be allowed to interfere with the primary goal of helping learners attain targeted valued capabilities, and if teachers are free to apply their judgments creatively concerning how best to develop those capabilities, then a healthy relationship to frame factors (Johnson, 1977) can be established.

Attention to the domains of learning has implications for instruction and assessment, as well as curriculum. Developing a passion for economic issues may require a very different method of instruction than developing a clear concept of opportunity cost, or skill in accounting, although all three may be attempted simultaneously in a coherent instructional fabric. In assessing attainment across the domains, we might focus on *how accurately* an idea is being represented or applied, *how effectively* a skill is exercised, and *how deeply* a disposition is experienced by the learner.

It is necessary to confront the mistaken notion that education is simply what teachers do. This notion inadvertently, but decisively, takes attention away from the student and what the student may be learning. Attention to the student can be maintained through a focus on assessment of learning outcomes aligned to learning goals. Some may be concerned that a focus on individual learning goals diverts attention from the learner to something that may turn out to be trivial. In actuality, a focus on learning goals clarifies our intentions, as well as our relationship to the learners, through attention to the development of their capabilities. *Knowing the Learner* places high value on the development of *core capabilities:* those capabilities that are productive for further learning and productivity in the world. Once the decision to value core capabilities is in place, the path opens to the possibility of empirical research that bears on the question of which capabilities actually *are* core capabilities.

Summary

Educational activities may be productively characterized as intentional efforts to develop valued human capabilities. This distinguishes education from accidental and unintentional learning. Clarity and precision in talking about education can then be facilitated by thinking in terms of intended learning outcomes or, more simply, learning goals. Thinking about educational activities in terms of learning goals makes possible precise definitions for the following key features of educational activities:

1. **Curriculum** — a structured set of learning goals

2. **Assessment** — information on how well the learning goals have been attained

3. **Instruction** — intentional efforts to directly influence the attainment of *learning goals*

4. **Evaluation** — the use of assessment (and other information) to understand and increase the value of all features of educational activities

What if we find an educational program operating without explicit learning goals or without assessment of how well the learning goals are being attained? How then is it possible to know whether its educational activities are succeeding? How can we know whether instruction is properly targeted, effective, and efficient? In fact, how can there be a sound basis for choosing any given method of instruction over another without knowing the learning goals? It is hard to imagine an educational program that has no instructional component, but without goals and assessment, instruction may well be ineffective, arbitrary, or a source of "mis-educative" experiences. The presence of learning goals and ways to tell how well the learning goals are being attained provide the necessary conditions for systematic evaluation and improvement in education.

CHAPTER III
What Is Educational Information?

Distinguishing educational from non-educational activities reveals a significant fact — that much of what takes place in educational institutions is not education at all! Similarly, much of the information that circulates in these institutions has no educational usefulness and can become a distraction from educational functions. True educational information is essentially quite simple and has wide applicability. Focusing primarily on this simple information opens the possibility of previously unimagined efficiency in supporting educational programs at any level, in any subject, and for any type of institution.

Chapter III
What Is Educational Information?

Give me a place to stand and with a lever I will move the whole world.

Archimedes of Syracuse

The Fulcrum of Educational Thinking and Action

Archimedes harnessed the power of the fulcrum as a conceptual as well as practical tool. Johnson's positing of the *intended learning outcome* or *learning goal* as the center point of thinking and action in education provided a foothold that allowed him to give precise meaning to *curriculum* and *instruction*. We have extended this idea further to give precise definition to *educational assessment*. These definitions can make the activities of educational assessment and evaluation more effective servants for reaching educational goals.

A Reminder Concerning Stipulated Definitions

For the sake of clarity and precision, and in order to make educational concepts efficiently serve educational purposes, we stipulate definitions for key terms such as *curriculum, assessment, instruction,* and *evaluation.* To be able to effectively follow the present discussion, it is necessary to abide by these definitions. We do not suggest that readers need adopt our definitions, except to try them out in the present context. We believe that the value of the distinctions associated with these definitions will demonstrate itself in practical application. A glossary of key terms is provided at the end of the book.

Educational and Non-Educational Activities

One of the themes of *Knowing the Learner* is the importance of distinguishing the educational from the non-educational activities that are found in educational programs. This distinction has allowed us to focus not only on the activities that are most important but also to avoid distractions that have no educational benefit and may even interfere with intended learning. The distinction is now pushed further to identify the essential *information* that is needed to support educational activities. What should that information be? How is it best collected, processed, and used? The answers to these questions become clear once the realization surfaces that what is needed is information that is immediately useful to teachers and learners as they go about their work.

What Is Educational Information?

The examination of educational assessment and evaluation presented in the preceding chapters revealed that educational information (i.e., information that serves strictly essential educational functions) centers on attention to how well individual learning goals have been attained. In fact, it is illuminating that the essential educational functions (*curriculum, assessment,* and *instruction*) can all be defined on the basis of the concept of the learning goal. In this chapter, we will consider the forms that this kind of information must take to be educationally productive and how to prevent the misuse of that information. As has already become evident, the most serious misuse of educational information is its application for non-educational purposes. This can distract attention from the goals for learning, dilute effectiveness of instruction, and produce deleterious side effects.

Practical Learning Goals That Are Specific and Distinct

The Critical Level of Specificity

Practical learning goals are intended learning outcomes specified at a level appropriate to planning, carrying out, and evaluating instruction. We call this the *critical level of specificity.* Practical learning goals are distinct from the learning goals that make up the common educational standards promulgated by state agencies. These *educational standards* are typically broad learning goals within which more specific learning goals are contained. Those who must take responsibility to design and carry out activities that help students attain such standards realize that working with broad goals is impractical and so break them down into more specific components. For example, the Education Department of the State of Georgia has identified **"Map and Globe Skills"** among its standards, and then more specific learning goals such as *"7. use a map to explain impact of geography on historical and current events"* and *"10. use graphic scales to determine distances on a map".*[9] Goals at the latter level of specificity are what is needed to plan instruction and build assessments.

Distinct (Discrete) Learning Goals

We have seen that the aggregation of information from disparate learning goals results in loss of educational usefulness. When building assessment in practical contexts then, the learning goals must have the property of being distinct from each other as well as specific. That means that one and only one practical learning goal is being addressed at a time.

---

[9] *https://www.georgiastandards.org/standards/GPS%20Support%20Docs/gps_Socialstudies_skills_matrix.pdf*

Because of the particular usefulness of the practical learning goal to instructional planning and evaluation, educational assessment is also best designed and carried out at this level of specificity and distinctiveness. Implementing standards always requires work at the level of goals that are distinct and specific. The term *learning objective* is often used to refer to the critical level of specificity of practical learning goals. However, there is sufficient variation and lack of precision in the use of the term learning objective that we find it productive to use the term *practical learning goals* instead and to refer to a *critical level of specificity*.

Practical Learning Outcomes

The critical unit of educational information then must be learning outcome information aligned to *practical learning goals*. Such information provides the most salient and useful basis for planning, carrying out, and evaluating instruction in practical educational settings, at the scenes of what we have referred to as educational events. This applies irrespective of whether the settings are classrooms, computer-based learning, or experiential learning activities. The outcome information aligned to a distinct learning goal at the critical level of specificity can be called the *practical learning outcome*.

What is not widely recognized is that practical learning outcome information is generalizable and can be useful on a large as well as a small scale. Not only is it the information most needed at the scene of educational events; we will show that it is, at the same time, the very information most needed for educational research, program evaluation, accountability, and decision-making at all levels of educational programs. This underlying multiple utility of the same information suggests the potential for a previously unimagined level of efficiency for educational information collection and use.

From the Student to the State

Educational assessments generate information about practical learning outcomes — information on how well practical learning goals have been attained. This is the primary information needed to support the work of teachers and learners at the scenes of educational events — the most vital level of the educational enterprise. Practical learning outcome information can be used to infer how well learning goals have been attained. This information provides the evidence needed to support planning, evaluation, and program improvement.

The following illustrations[10] are intended to demonstrate how the degree of attainment of *practical learning outcomes* can serve information needs at all levels of educational systems. Examples are drawn from an assessment activity known as **Cubes and Liquids**.[11]

Figure 3.1 shows how the level of attainment on a learning goal can be depicted visually. We chose to characterize the lowest level as ***no evidence*** *of attainment* rather than as ***no*** *attainment* because of the inherent limitations of educational assessment. Assessment can elicit and present evidence concerning how well a learning goal has been attained, but cannot tell us definitively that a student has *not* attained a particular learning goal. At best, we can say that we have found no evidence of attainment. Failure to obtain evidence of attainment could be a result of faulty or ineffective assessment practices as well as student non-attainment. For visual simplicity, two levels — "attained" and "proficient" — have been combined, although, under certain conditions, these might be profitably distinguished. Indeed, levels might be characterized with even finer distinctions where appropriate for particular learning goals.

---

[10] *The graphics that follow are not based on analysis of real data. Rather, they are heuristic simulations illustrating ways in which practical learning outcomes can serve as the information needed for planning, evaluation, resource allocation, and accountability at all levels of educational programs. A working version of this system exists, however, and can be adjusted to function at all the levels that will be shown.*

[11] *http://acase.org/cubes-liquids/*

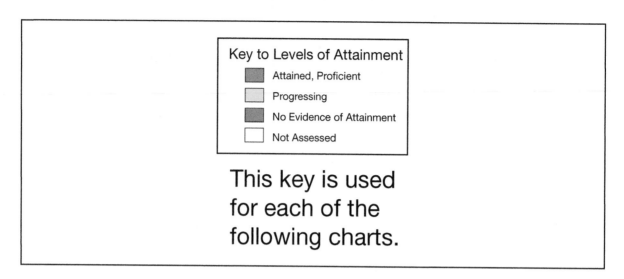

Figure 3.1 Key to levels of attainment for a practical learning outcome

The levels of student performance on a single learning goal can then be displayed for a single class as in **Figure 3.2**. The display provides the teacher with detailed information about the number and percentage of individuals performing at each level. Performance information is aggregated across students while discrete information about the learning goal is maintained. A teacher can use such information to gauge overall attainment for an entire class. Corresponding reports can be generated to compare any groups within the class.

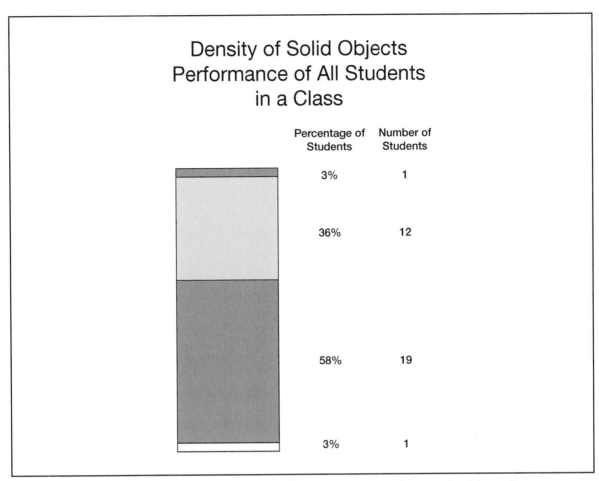

Figure 3.2 Performance of all students in a class on a single practical learning outcome

Teachers need to consider the attainments of individual students as well as overall class progress for any given learning goal as instruction progresses. **Figure 3.3** contains a report of individual student outcome information over time for a single learning goal. A ninth grade teacher has chosen to display the performance of all of her students on measures of **density of solid objects** at the beginning and midpoint of the school year in order to plan how she will address this learning goal during the remaining portion of the year. She also called up information on how these same students were performing on the learning goal before they entered her class (in this case, at the end of the eighth grade). **Figure 3.3** contains a sample of individual student performance outcomes to illustrate that it is possible to consider the class and individuals at the same time. In this case, she chose to display assessment results for all of her students, but she might also have generated a report for the classes separately to see if they differed in any substantial way. The top portion of the figure moves from left to right displaying class performance on this learning goal over time. Progress in attaining this learning goal is indicated by the increasing raw values and percentages of students represented in green and yellow. The bottom portion of the figure illustrates how the detailed information on individual students can be represented as well as the group as a whole.

Thus, the progress of individual students on a learning goal can be easily viewed at any point in time up to the most recent date of assessment. Imagine that teachers need not wait for the end of unit, quarter, semester, or year for such reports, but can obtain this type of assessment information whenever they need it. Such reports are simple and practical, and such timeliness is within the purview of current information technologies. A report in this form allows the teacher to give special attention and differential instruction to individual students based on their current levels of attainment, as well as to prepare an overall instructional strategy for groups. Similar reports can be generated in near real time to study potential differences in performance for any identifiable subgroup — for example, students who have received different instructional treatments or to see if boys are responding to instruction in the same way as girls.

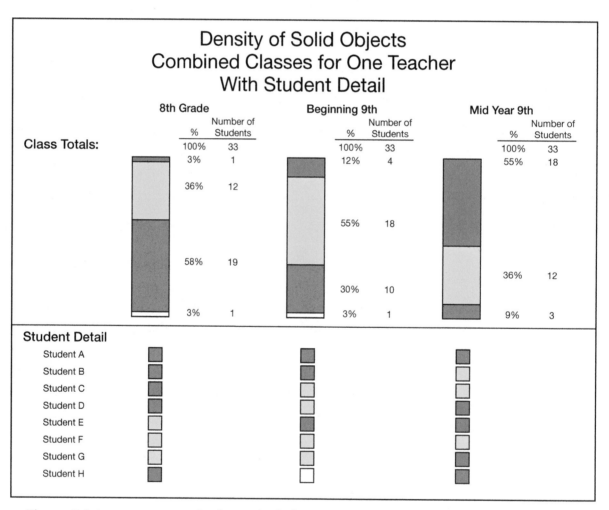

Figure 3.3 Assessment results for a single learning goal for combined classes over time

Supervisors and administrators can generate similar reports to monitor district-wide progress within and across grade levels for learning goals of interest over any period of time desired **(Figure 3.4)**. These reports would be based on exactly the same information that was used by teachers for instructional planning, namely assessment data on how well students attained practical learning goals. Increase in the green and yellow portions of the displays from left to right signifies growth in attainment. White indicates that assessments were not conducted. Blank portions of the figure indicate that attention has turned away from assessing some learning goals, perhaps because a sufficient level of attainment has been attained overall in the mind of the user. Note that the aggregation is always across students on a single learning goal. This is completely different from the aggregation across diverse learning goals that characterizes conventional tests and grades.

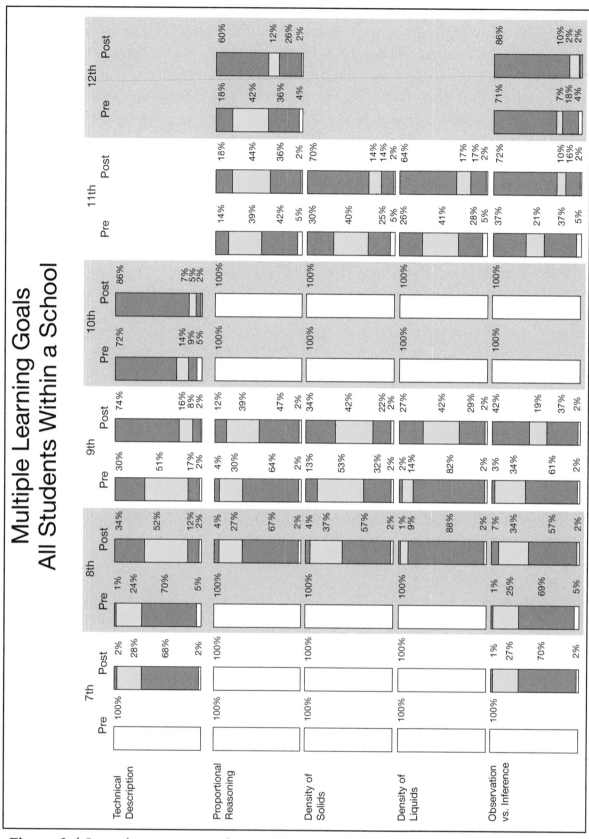

Figure 3.4 Learning outcomes for multiple practical learning outcomes, school or district wide, aggregation: all students by grade level

This type of presentation can be extended further to support planning for entire school districts and even larger entities. **Figure 3.5** demonstrates how precisely the same information on individual student attainment of practical learning outcomes can be productive for planning and evaluation at every level from the classroom to the state. What is presented in **Figure 3.5** is the kind and use of information that is missing from most analyses of educational data. But to serve as the basis for the type of constructive decision-making described here, the information must be maintained in terms of how well discrete learning goals are being attained! If the targeted capabilities are core capabilities, such focus in no way gives too much attention to a small set of learning goals.

Note that one class has surpassed school, district, and state performance levels by mid-ninth grade, even though it began with a typical profile. Students in this class seem to have progressed more rapidly than students at all other institutional levels in spite of the fact that their performance was more or less uniform at the outset. Such a finding suggests the existence of a factor that has positively affected attainment related to the targeted learning goal. Could this factor be associated with something that the teacher is doing? If so, is there something that can be learned from this teacher by other teachers across the district and the state having to do with realizing the targeted learning goal? Can this teacher become a resource for professional development for the school, the district, the state? The results for the school suggest the possibility that this may already be happening locally.

Deliberation concerning such unexpected goal attainment can be useful at all levels. Such evidence can provide a basis for decisions concerning professional development and resource allocation. The evaluative application of this information can lead to needed resources being directed to areas where individuals and groups are performing below expectations or to glean resources (e.g., expertise) from settings that are experiencing particular success. Thus, constructive rather than punitive actions can be the main line of follow-up for those who are concerned with accountability. Non-oppressive means can be applied to support the aims of state initiatives such as *No Child Left Behind* and *Every Student Succeeds.*

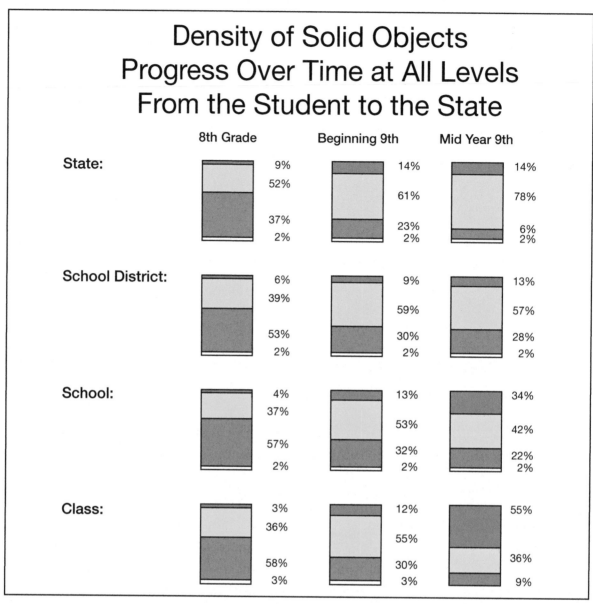

Figure 3.5 Aggregation at all levels from the student to the state

Thus, the same unit of information (i.e., practical learning outcomes aligned to practical learning goals) is available for purposes of instructional planning, evaluation, resource allocation, professional development, and even accountability at all levels of educational institutions. Such information is simple, to the point, and immediately meaningful and appropriate for decision-making and action on the part of teachers, students, parents, supervisors, evaluation specialists, policymakers, and legislators — in other words, at all levels from the student to the state. This makes possible a virtually unparalleled efficiency in collection and use of educational information. Moreover, it is *the* information that is most salient for all of these purposes at all those levels.

Reports and inference of this kind do not require the arcane methods for scaling, analysis, and reporting that currently characterize the work of state education agencies and the testing industry when they construct and report on tests. The fixation with cutoff scores, item difficulty, and elaborate scaling and analysis methods that has dominated educational measurement for a century has stemmed from their history of association with high-stakes, norm-referenced (HSNR) testing and grading. The focus concomitant with the HSNR tradition has been on ranking, comparing, and discrimination of students — and more recently of teachers — all for non-educational purposes! This tradition has exacted an immense cost from the educational enterprise with little or no educational benefit. It does not take long after examining any of the almost-omnipresent HSNR tests and methods, and the way they are applied, to see that they have little to do with helping people teach or learn.

Thus, action at the level of the educational event can be supported and its value increased in various ways through action from other levels. Schools, school districts, state agencies, and professional organizations can all provide support in the form of professional development and resources based on practical learning outcome information. Practical learning outcomes can meet the information needs of all these levels and, in fact, can do so more effectively and efficiently than any other information currently used for these purposes.

Vital Signs for Educational Programs

With reports such as the ones displayed above, students, teachers, schools, and school communities can know at all times not only which students are not progressing but precisely what they are failing to attain. This gives the direction needed for teachers and the school community to take targeted action. It makes clear what students and teachers are accomplishing or failing to accomplish. It is the necessary information basis for productive planning. Imagine that a school community has identified a set of learning goals (say 20 or 25) that are considered critical for all students to attain by the time they complete a certain grade. Reports illustrating progress with respect to learning outcomes related to those goals could be viewed as in **Figure 3.5**. A version that shows individual student performance at each point could easily be generated as well. Limiting the number of learning goals to those that are most important is the key to keeping such data from becoming overwhelming. Such reports focusing on core capabilities can become the *vital signs* of an educational program.

How Vital Information Can Be Missing

Unfortunately, the centrality — indeed, necessity — for information on student attainment to be distinct and specific in order for it to serve planning and decision-making at policy as well as instructional levels is not generally recognized. Take as a case in point a recent policy study published by the National Research Council: *Monitoring Progress Toward Successful K-12 STEM Education: A Nation Advancing?* (National Research Council of the National Academies, 2013). This study was solicited as follow-up on an earlier report (National Research Council of the National

Academies, 2011) that offered recommendations for promoting successful K-12 education in science, technology, engineering, and mathematics (STEM). The 2013 study was commissioned to identify methods for tracking progress related to these successful programs. Fourteen indicators were developed (National Research Council of the National Academies, 2011, p. 2). Disappointingly, only one of the indicators relates to educational assessment, and that one monitors "States' use of assessments that measure the core concepts and practices of science and mathematics disciplines," rather than obtaining actual information on student attainment. In other words, tracking of progress in the STEM education disciplines would be carried out without including a direct report on attainment of learning goals (e.g., Common Core and NGSS standards). Success would be monitored and discussed without looking at student learning outcomes. This state of affairs is not unusual and perhaps it is what the education community has come to expect, but how can we monitor progress in educational programs — how can we confirm the success of educational programs — if we do not have reports on what was and was not attained and by whom? What does the proposed study provide that will help support teachers in helping their students attain the learning goals for which they and the students will be held responsible? This suggests a serious disconnect between research and policy enterprises and the needs of teachers and learners.

Foundations for Productive Educational Data Analysis Already Exist

It is understandable that data from conventional HSNR are not a useful basis for monitoring program progress and success, but credible and useful alternative methodologies are available. Respected technologies for educational assessment used by agencies such as *The National Assessment of Educational Progress* (NAEP)[12], the *Trends in International Mathematics and Science Study* (TIMSS)[13], and the *Programme for International Student Assessment* (PISA)[14] exist and represent alternative models for reporting student attainment. These assessments collect and can report information on student attainment at the level of practical learning outcomes and are all explicitly concerned with the issue underlying the identification of core capabilities. Such assessment technologies could and should be used to monitor progress related to any educational initiative. Monitoring progress in the attainment of practical learning goals over time is the most direct and telling way, indeed the necessary way, to tell if instruction is succeeding.

---

[12] *http://nces.ed.gov/nationsreportcard/*

[13] *http://timssandpirls.bc.edu/about.html*

[14] *https://www.oecd.org/pisa/*

Is Aggregation Across Diverse Learning Goals Necessarily Inappropriate?

All of the preceding examples have referred to performance measures in which student information has been aggregated within discrete learning goals. The problems with aggregating across diverse learning goals have been pointed out several times. We cautioned against aggregating information across diverse learning goals because of the concomitant loss of educational information. However, it can be useful to aggregate over diverse learning goals when they are in related subject matter. Indeed, thoughtful aggregation and disaggregation can be the key to moving up and down between broad learning goals (e.g., the typical *standards*) and practical learning goals and outcomes.

An example can be found in the reports that follow. They are from AGEO 110, "The Search for Life Beyond the Earth," a course in astrobiology offered by the Department of Atmospheric and Environmental Sciences at the University at Albany as part of the Natural Science component in the University's General Education Program. The instructor, Professor John W. Delano, used pre/post surveys and clickers as means for obtaining outcome information to plan upcoming instruction. The examples that follow concentrate on a portion of the course curriculum devoted to understanding conditions that need to be in place in a planetary system for it to support life. **Figure 3.6** presents a form used by a rater to indicate which of the learning goals associated with *Conditions Needed for Life to Occur* were attained. The form displays the full set of 12 distinct (though related) learning goals for this topic. The reports that follow illustrate the potential usefulness of aggregation across learning goals but also its limitations. The full set of practical learning goals for the course and the assessment instrument to which students responded are presented in Appendix C and D, respectively.

Conditions for Life-Restricted Temperature range (LifeCon-A) ❷	◉ 1. Refers to Restricted Temperature range ○ 0. No evidence of attainment ○ Not Rated
Conditions for Life-Restricted Pressure range (LifeCon-B) ❷	○ 1. Refers to Restricted Pressure range ◉ 0. No evidence of attainment ○ Not Rated
Conditions for Life-Sources(s) of nutrients (LifeCon-C) ❷	◉ 1. Refers to Source(s) of Nutrients ○ 0. No evidence of attainment ○ Not Rated
Conditions for Life-Geological times (LifeCon-D) ❷	○ 1. Refers to Geological times ◉ 0. No evidence of attainment ○ Not Rated
Conditions for Life-Planet/Satellite system (LifeCon-E) ❷	○ 1. Refers to Planet/Satellite system ◉ 0. No evidence of attainment ○ Not Rated
Conditions for Life-Liquid water (LifeCon-F) ❷	◉ 1. Refers to Liquid water ○ 0. No evidence of attainment ○ Not Rated
Conditions for Life-Synthesis of molecules for life's function (e.g., DNA and RNA analogs) (LifeCon-G) ❷	○ 1. Refers to Synthesis of molecules for life's function ◉ 0. No evidence of attainment ○ Not Rated
Conditions for Life-Absence of (or protection against) planet-sterilizing events (LifeCon-H) ❷	◉ 1. Refers to Absence of (or protection against) planet-sterilizing events ○ 0. No evidence of attainment ○ Not Rated
Conditions for Life-Object of 0.5-5.0 Earth mass (LifeCon-I) ❷	○ 1. Refers to Object of 0.5-5.0 Earth mass ◉ 0. No evidence of attainment ○ Not Rated
Conditions for Life-Habitable/Goldilocks zone (LifeCon-J) ❷	◉ 1. Refers to Habitable/Goldilocks zone ○ 0. No evidence of attainment ○ Not Rated
Conditions for Life-Long-lived, stable star (LifeCon-K) ❷	○ 1. Refers to Long-lived, stable star ◉ 0. No evidence of attainment ○ Not Rated
Conditions for Life-Terrestrial vs. Extra T (LifeCon-L) ❷	○ 1. Refers to Terrestrial vs. Extra T ◉ 0. No evidence of attainment ○ Not Rated

Figure 3.6 Distinct learning goals associated with *Conditions Needed for Life to Occur*

Figure 3.7 displays assessment results indicating how many of the *conditions for life* learning goals were attained by students in the class on each of two different occasions. This constitutes an aggregation across the 12 learning goals, as well as across all of the students in the class.

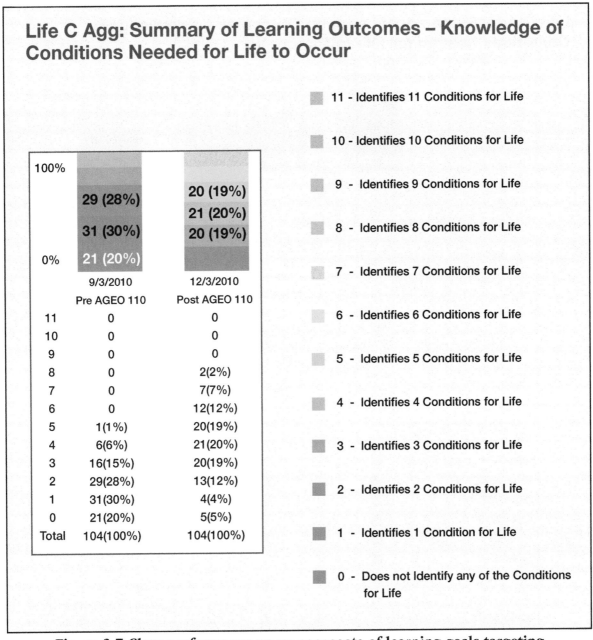

Life C Agg: Summary of Learning Outcomes – Knowledge of Conditions Needed for Life to Occur

	11 - Identifies 11 Conditions for Life
	10 - Identifies 10 Conditions for Life
	9 - Identifies 9 Conditions for Life
	8 - Identifies 8 Conditions for Life
	7 - Identifies 7 Conditions for Life
	6 - Identifies 6 Conditions for Life
	5 - Identifies 5 Conditions for Life
	4 - Identifies 4 Conditions for Life
	3 - Identifies 3 Conditions for Life
	2 - Identifies 2 Conditions for Life
	1 - Identifies 1 Condition for Life
	0 - Does not Identify any of the Conditions for Life

	9/3/2010 Pre AGEO 110	12/3/2010 Post AGEO 110
11	0	0
10	0	0
9	0	0
8	0	2(2%)
7	0	7(7%)
6	0	12(12%)
5	1(1%)	20(19%)
4	6(6%)	21(20%)
3	16(15%)	20(19%)
2	29(28%)	13(12%)
1	31(30%)	4(4%)
0	21(20%)	5(5%)
Total	104(100%)	104(100%)

Figure 3.7 Class performance on an aggregate of learning goals targeting knowledge of *Conditions Needed for Life to Occur*

Figure 3.8 provides additional information. It contains a color-coded representation of how many learning goals were attained by a sample of individual students. The instructor can use such reports, in which diverse learning goals that have common content are aggregated, in order to see whether portions of the curriculum may need special attention. However, when it comes time to plan, carry out, and evaluate instruction (i.e., to work at the level of critical specificity), it is necessary to look at the results by the distinct, practical learning outcomes, as is illustrated in **Figure 3.9**.

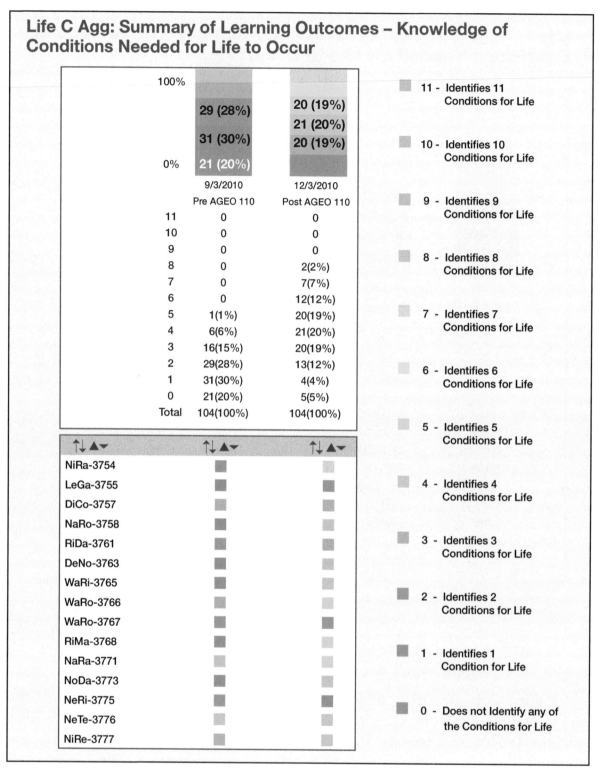

Figure 3.8 Class and individual student performance on an aggregate of learning goals targeting knowledge of *Conditions Needed for Life to Occur*

Figure 3.9 displays performance on two of the component learning goals in the *Conditions Needed for Life to Occur* curriculum. A look at the lower half of **Figure 3.9** reveals that the aggregate report (**Figure 3.8**) obscures the fact that there is no evidence of student attainment on either occasion for the learning goal that addresses synthesis of molecules in life functions. Only with reports on distinct learning goals can the instructor consider the practical implications of assessment results. With information at the level of distinct learning goals, many practical questions can begin to be well directed. Was insufficient attention given to providing instruction targeted to this learning goal? Did instruction fail to target the goal properly? Did the assessment method fail to elicit evidence of student attainment? Has the instructor simply not yet addressed this learning goal?

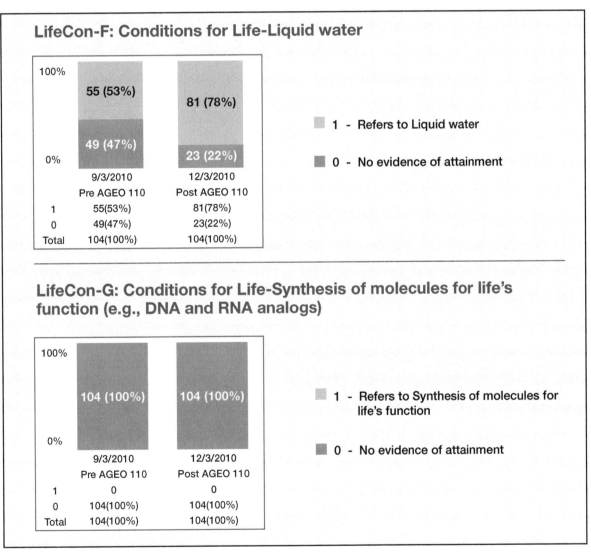

Figure 3.9 Class attainment on two selected practical learning outcomes from the *Conditions Needed for Life to Occur* curriculum

Aggregated assessment results can be very useful. The NAEP often presents reports on growth or decline of student performance in broad topics like algebra or mathematics, or compares the performance of different demographic groups in these areas. But, for practical educational purposes, it is always necessary to turn attention back to the specific items that give information concerning practical learning outcomes.

Aggregation and Accomplishment-Based Grading

The situation regarding aggregation of substantially different sources of information creates a parallel problem in the case of assigning grades. Institutions that demand grades from teachers specify that those grades be a single number or letter. Inevitably, such values become sapped of objective meaning and usefulness. This is in part because of variations in the criteria used for assigning grades by different teachers and schools, but also because of the subjective factors at work in assigning grades. With accomplishment-based grading, as we have defined it, the components of the grading process can be made explicit and transparent and carried out objectively. But there is always the problem of interpretation of unitary score values derived by aggregation across diverse tasks. What can be legitimately inferred concerning the aggregate grade itself in the case of accomplishment-based grading as presented in Chapter I? Simply how well students have succeeded in meeting the requirements set by the teacher. If the underlying tasks were properly designed, properly scored, and aggregated, they reveal the degree to which the student is willing and able to successfully complete tasks that are designed to promote learning. These are significant pieces of information for prospective employers and postsecondary institutions. Teachers and school decision makers for their own purposes, however, need to be able to look at the components of a grade separately, and these components need to be made available to those interested in a finer-grained picture of student accomplishments. Similarly, reports on attainment of practical learning outcomes and aggregates of learning outcomes within unified content areas can be presented as illustrated in the *conditions of life* example.

Implications

It is worth considering the case of W. Edwards Deming who, in the aftermath of the Second World War, advised the captains of Japanese industry that adopting the method of statistical process control would make Japanese manufacturing internationally competitive. We believe that those who grasp the implications of Johnson's model of educational processes and learn to apply information based on the assessment of *practical learning goals aligned with core capabilities* can similarly discover new efficiency in their educational work, which will leave conventional programs behind. This may happen with individual teachers, with schools, with businesses, through educational video games, indeed in any educational program.

Navigating around unproductive institutional features and focusing on the attainment of *core capabilities* will allow those educational practitioners who do so to set a path of leadership in the midst of the chaotic conditions of information that characterize contemporary educational decision making.

Summary

Understanding what is being accomplished in educational programs at all levels has been obscured through use of the wrong information (aggregated test scores) and evaluation of programs has become unproductive and even destructive through misuse of that information. Such are the consequences of the practices of high-stakes, norm-referenced testing and grading. The aggregated scores associated with high-stakes, norm-referenced tests and grades produce information that cannot be used productively to understand, evaluate, and improve educational activities.

Meaningful educational information is inherent in and founded on the alignment of learning outcomes with their associated learning goals. Learning goals provide a way to imagine and think about the capabilities to be developed. Distinct learning outcome information provides evidence of how well those learning goals were attained.

All educational decisions are ultimately justified by their relationship to learning goals and learning outcomes. The central unit of information for understanding and taking productive action in educational activities is the practical learning outcome. Practical learning outcomes are aligned with practical learning goals that, by definition, should be distinct (unaggregated). Practical learning goals and outcomes should also be defined at the *critical level of specificity* — the level of specificity appropriate for planning, carrying out, and evaluating instruction. Looked at from another point of view, to be useful to teachers and learners at the scene of educational events, information needs to be at the level of the practical learning outcome.

Moreover, educational research, evaluation, questions of resource allocation and professional development, policy analysis and decision-making, theories of instruction, and questions of accountability — all of these are best addressed and carried out when grounded in learning outcome information on the attainment of learning goals that is collected, analyzed, and presented at the level of the practical learning outcome.

To the degree that information in educational programs departs from practical learning outcomes, it loses value for educational purposes. The essential purpose of educational activities is the movement from learning goals to learning outcomes. Educational activities are most productive and effective when they are carried out at the level of practical learning goals and outcomes.

CHAPTER IV
What Is *Good* Educational Information?

Traditionally, the question of the quality of educational information has been the exclusive domain of specialists in educational assessment, evaluation, and research. But, in reality, this question is a central concern for of *all* participants and stakeholders in the educational process — teachers, supervisors, policymakers, parents, and even students. Teachers in particular can be empowered and prepared to take greater responsibility for the quality of the information they use and how they use it. This in turn will help to make educational assessment and evaluation more accountable servants of educational goals.

Chapter IV
What Is Good Educational Information?

It seems clear that whatever happens with external, imposed assessment...a key direction for the future lies in the development of teachers' classroom assessment skills.

(Gipps, 1999, p. 387)

It was a critical moment in scientific history when Johannes Kepler decided to abandon his model of the solar system, a model in which planets orbited in circles around an off-center sun (Feynman, 1965). Kepler noticed that the position of the planet Mars predicted by his model differed by a small, but substantial, amount from the observations of his predecessor Tycho Brahe. Kepler's confidence in the accuracy of Tycho's observations was so great that he concluded that even such a small difference could not be ignored. Kepler's own work was carried out at a great level of precision and this, matched by his confidence in the reliability of Tycho's work, led him to reject his own theory and move to other ones, leading finally to the presently held model of elliptical planetary orbits. Can we achieve such a level of confidence in our deliberations and pronouncements concerning what is taking place in educational programs? Are not the stakes of attainment of human capabilities at least as high? How can we begin to build sound information about educational attainment?

Assessment is education's information function. It reveals evidence for how well intended learning outcomes are being attained. The desirable properties of educational assessments can be identified by means of four questions.

- Does assessment information truly correspond to the learning goals?

- Is the assessment information dependable?

- Is the information available when and where it is needed?

- Is the information worth the effort of collecting?

We may characterize these as the questions of *validity, reliability, timeliness,* and *efficiency* of assessment information, respectively.

Educational vs. Non-Educational Measurement

In spite of its extensive misuse in educational programs, conventional measurement theory in education and the social sciences (often referred to as *psychometrics*) has made a notable contribution to a theory of educational information. It has done so by emphasizing the necessity that assessment instruments be valid and reliable. However, because the field of measurement, as it is presently applied in educational practice, has been operating almost exclusively with composite tests consisting of aggregations of information from diverse learning goals rather than information on the attainment of distinct, practical learning outcomes, a new approach to these two central concepts is needed. Considerations of validity and reliability that can have truly educational import must necessarily differ from those that characterize conventional testing practices. Educational conceptions of validity and reliability must be appropriate to practical learning goals and outcomes, and so will look very different from those that are applied in conventional measurement in educational programs. By and large, what has been called *educational measurement* is not educational in nature or application at all, as evidenced by non-educational practices such as ranking and scaling measures of student attainment and the policies of grading on a curve.

It is critical in approaching this subject to dispense with the notion that validity and reliability are concepts that are too technical or too difficult for teachers to grasp and use appropriately. This point of view is simply an example of demeaning the image and role of teachers, something all too common among many of today's policymakers and educational specialists. Every time a teacher or a student (or anyone for that matter) raises the question of whether a test or test item really measures what it should be measuring, they are raising the question of *validity*! It is a concern for everyone. Moreover, the need for validity has an eminently practical purpose. Pamela Moss expresses the requirements from a teacher's practical perspective in her article *Reconceptualizing Validity for Classroom Assessment*:

> *What I need to do is make decisions — moment-to-moment, day-to-day, course-to-course — that help students learn, as individuals and as members of learning communities and to study the effects of my decisions.*

(Moss, 2003)

The primary reason why teachers have been little interested in the concepts of validity and reliability to date is that the concepts have referred almost exclusively to aggregates of diverse learning goals — as in high-stakes, norm-referenced tests — and so have not been of use in practical instructional planning and evaluation.

Validity Reconsidered

Does an assessment instrument really measure what it purports to? How do we know? These are the essential questions that characterize concern for *validity*. Validity must always be a central question in the mind of anyone who examines an assessment procedure or its results. One of the reasons why the conventional realization of the concept of validity has not been a more integral part of teacher concerns is that it does not speak directly to the specifics of the teaching-learning process. The first step that must be taken to make the concept of validity a helpful one for educational activities is to focus it at the level of practical learning goals. For this reason, again, much of the rich body of research and theory that has been carried out historically can be of only limited value.

When considering the validity of an assessment instrument or activity, we are primarily interested in whether its component practical learning outcomes correspond to their associated practical learning goals and provide sound evidence that the underlying targeted capabilities are being attained. Establishing the nature of the underlying capability warrants serious empirical study in its own right because capabilities as such are not directly observable; they must be inferred on the basis of evidence from assessments. W. James Popham makes this clear in saying, "...what is *most important* [Popham's emphasis]... is not what goes on inside a classroom, but what goes on *inside a teacher's head and inside a student's head*" (Popham, 2011, p. 11). Robert Mislevy touches on the essence of the issue in pointing out that "... the heart of test theory is connecting what we can observe with a more general, inherently unobservable, concept of what a student knows and can do" (Mislevy, 1993, p. ix).[15] The *learning goals* that we speak of in *Knowing the Learner* refer specifically to such targeted capabilities.

In contemporary educational practice, the goodness of fit between learning goal and learning outcome on the one hand, and the targeted capability on the other is customarily determined by expert judgment. Standardized assessments of discrete learning goals are typically developed by teams of content experts and measurement specialists. Frameworks are developed which state the theoretical basis for the assessment methods and provide directions for the kinds of tasks that will characterize the assessments, as well as how they should be designed. Experts in the subject matter decide whether particular assessment items[16] are to be considered valid. This has been the way of doing things for a century now. It is time to move to the next evolutionary step in establishing validity. Goodness of fit will need to be established empirically — that is, through scientific investigation. One way to do this is to find out the degree to which measures of the same capability agree. Validity can also be established by studying sequences of attainment among different capabilities. The idea of *learning progressions* points to such a possibility.

---

[15] *The question of the goodness of fit between an assessment and an underlying capability is a concern that has a rich history of theory and research under the rubric of construct validity (Kane, 2006). The central psychological construct in education is the underlying capability associated with the practical learning goal or learning outcome.*

[16] *Specific tasks that **test** takers are asked to perform, e.g., multiple-choice questions*

By its very nature, learning involves progression. To assist in its emergence, teachers need to understand the pathways along which students are expected to progress. These pathways or progressions ground both instruction and assessment. Yet, despite a plethora of standards and curricula, many teachers are unclear about how learning progresses in specific domains. This is an undesirable situation for teaching and learning, and one that particularly affects teachers' ability to engage in formative assessment.

(Heritage, 2008)

The problem that Margaret Heritage poses actually heralds the opening of a great opportunity for establishing validity of assessment items. If dependable measures of attainment of discrete learning goals can be developed, then we can investigate how their respective learning outcomes might be related to each other. Which are dependent on others? Which are supportive of others? Can chains of dependency between learning outcomes be established that would suggest an order for curriculum and instruction? A study of the relationships between capabilities at the level at which teaching and learning take place should be one of the top items on the agenda of educational research. It would provide the basis for identifying and validating learning progressions and for filling in the needed pieces in "curriculum's missing database" (Johnson, 1985). If progressions of learning outcomes can be established, it will be possible to identify when students have become stuck at a certain point in their development and to target instruction to remedy the situation. Of course, this information would have to be at the level of distinct and specific practical learning goals and outcomes. Such a line of research could also become the basis for identifying and establishing core capabilities.

Classroom teachers typically do not have the benefit of content area and test design specialists to advise them in constructing their assessments and so they must rely on their own judgment and experience and, if fortunate enough, those of their colleagues. But what if teachers could have access to assessment instruments constructed by such specialists for the learning goals they are targeting? Such instruments exist. They are items that have been developed, tested, and administered in prestigious national and international assessments such as the National Assessment of Educational Progress (NAEP),[17] the Program for International Student Assessment (PISA),[18] and the Trends in International Mathematics and Science Study (TIMSS).[19]

---

[17] *http://nces.ed.gov/nationsreportcard/geography/*

[18] *http://www.oecd.org/pisa/aboutpisa/*

[19] *https://nces.ed.gov/timss/*

Items on these assessments are developed, collected, and reported at the level of practical learning goals, and so could be useful to teachers in cases where they correspond to the learning goals in their curricula. The frameworks for building these national and international assessments are already geared towards looking for capabilities of central importance, something very much like what we are calling core capabilities. Indeed, in the United States, many teachers have access to excellent assessment items developed by their own states in alignment with the learning goals that are typically called *standards*. The benefits to students, teachers, and schools of using such assessment items are many. For example, they would be able to compare local performance on a critical item with provincial, national, and international performance of students at the same age level. This would not be for the purpose of inciting competition (although competition is not necessarily bad), but rather to show what is possible for students to attain at various developmental levels. At the scene of an educational event, we want to be confident in the soundness of information concerning how well targeted learning goals have been attained by students. Having access to varieties of validated assessment items for given learning goals will help to justify such confidence. All the better if assessment items for the same learning goal have been developed by different sources. "Having multiple sources of evidence gathered across time and situation enhances the validity of an interpretation" (Moss, 2003).

Increasingly, the measurement community has broadened the question of validity from whether an assessment test really measures what it intends, to whether assessment results are being properly used (American Educational Research Association (AERA), American Psychological Association (APA), & National Council on Measurement in Education (NCME), 2014). This consideration has arisen primarily because of the damaging effects of high-stakes, norm-referenced testing and grading and other non-educational uses of assessment information. The notions of assessment and evaluation presented in *Knowing the Learner* are directed strictly and exclusively to the purposes of supporting learning and improving the fundamental educational activities. In this case, the question of whether assessment results are being used appropriately is sufficiently addressed.

The appropriate use of assessment instruments has also been of issue because of the ways that assessment outcomes differ between different populations of learners. But if an assessment item is valid, if the learning goal is appropriate for the student and if the resulting information is being used strictly to help the student attain the learning goal, then there is no need to fear differential scores for different populations. Undoubtedly, students with different demographic backgrounds (gender, cultural background, socioeconomic status) will respond differently to assessment items. For this, among other reasons, it is important to have multiple measures of every learning goal and to study differential performance by different populations. Having diverse means of assessing a learning goal and comparing the performances of different groups is a means for identifying the presence of cultural biases in assessment instruments.

Our aim should be to see to it that members of every targeted population are helped to attain the learning goal. The overall picture then reverses dramatically. We want to employ assessment instruments on populations of interest that are performing differentially. Results from these assessments can lead both to ways to serve those populations better and to produce more effective assessments.

A broad summary of the dilemmas associated with applying the classical concept of validity to practical educational contexts is provided by Daniel Koretz in his book *Measuring Up* (Koretz, 2008). But these problems essentially dissolve when the main theme of validity becomes establishing the goodness of fit between practical learning goals and outcomes on the one hand and the targeted underlying capabilities to which they refer on the other, and when the resulting information is applied strictly for educational purposes. In this light, we can put most of the contemporary concerns for appropriateness of use of assessment results aside and deal directly with the question of whether a method of assessment truly gets at the essence of what was intended to be learned, i.e., what has historically been called *construct validity*.

Reliability in Practical Application

Information needs to be dependable. The concept of *reliability* is directed towards establishing the dependability of measurement instruments. Reliability is often thought of in terms of obtaining consistent results from repeated measures of some phenomenon or obtaining agreement among independent observations of a phenomenon. Jeffrey Smith has highlighted the inappropriateness of conventional measures of reliability for useful application in educational activities and the difficulties of providing useful educational conceptions of reliability (Smith, 2003). Why these two problems are the case is not generally understood, however. The underlying reason is primarily that the concept of reliability has not yet been brought to the support of educational activities at the level of practical learning goals.

There are many ways to establish reliability of an instrument. We will focus on one method that has great potential for supporting educational activities. Measurement specialists often refer to it as *inter-rater reliability*. Reliability is typically the purview of test developers and educational researchers, but here we suggest that there is great value for teachers in grasping and taking advantage of this concept for themselves. Let's approach the concept of reliability by looking for consistency in judgments made regarding the level of attainment of practical learning goals.

Imagine examples of student performance that are rated blindly (i.e., with the identity of students hidden, so as to overcome potential bias in judgment). Let's say the teacher rates the exact same examples on two different occasions. We expect the teacher would give the same rating both times to the exact same object of attention. If not, we should consider two possibilities: 1) the teacher was not careful in making judgments, 2) the criteria for rating were not properly established (e.g., not properly standardized). We can go further and ask several teachers to rate these same samples of student performance. Disagreement among several raters gives additional opportunity to discover whether the two problems identified are occurring. Disagreement may also be an indication that either the assessment activity or the rating procedure is not valid. In that case, occasions of inconsistency of ratings can direct a teacher's attention to make appropriate corrections in the assessment instrument in order to improve validity. If the scoring is not blind, there is always an additional hypothesis to consider and that is that the teacher's ratings may be biased. The phenomenon of disagreement in and of itself provides powerful information!

When teachers or any group of individuals agree in their ratings of student attainment, we can speak of having a *reliable* method of rating. Generally speaking, the validity and reliability of classroom assessments is assumed (typically, it is not even considered) by the teacher and educational program. But these assumptions can actually be confronted objectively. What if a group of teachers do not agree in their ratings? **Figure 4.1** displays actual data on how well a group of teachers agreed in their ratings of the *engagement value* of stories submitted by students. The "standard" rating in the first column is the one made by the person who developed the criteria and organized the study (typically, the teacher). Values in black font color signify ratings that are in agreement with the standard. Red font indicates disagreement with the standard. Rating procedures of this kind can serve several purposes. In the present case, there is sufficient irregularity of agreement to warrant serious consideration of the rating criterion and/or the rating instructions. Perhaps the teacher who developed the rating scale needs to give more detailed instructions or examples for each of the levels on the rating scale. Note in particular the first rating, in which the "guest" teachers agree with each other but not with the standard. When the basis for what we have called here the "standard" rating has been made explicit and tested previously so that it leads to high levels of agreement, then this method of displaying agreement of ratings can be used to train others to learn how to use the rating procedures correctly. A display of this sort can highlight instances where rating procedures are not being used correctly and can give indications of bias as well, e.g., when a rater consistently gives high or low ratings. A technical report on the assessment activity **Cubes and Liquids** is available that documents the use of this technique to improve the rating procedures for that assessment instrument.[20]

---

[20] *http://acase.org/cubes-liquids/technical-report/*

Reliability Ratings
Engagement Value of Story

3 Engaging throughout.
2 Engaging for the most part.
1 Engaging in parts.
0 Not engaging at all.
N Not Rated

Raters are included only if they have at least one rating for this assessment. To see a list of all raters, edit the class in a new window.

To open a new window with just one rater's ratings, click the rater's name in the column header.

To see a student's self rating view, return to your grid and choose self reliability for that student.

Non-matches are red.

Student	Standard	Teacher Two	Teacher One	Teacher Three	Percent Match
09, 09	2	1	1	1	0.0%
11, 11	2	2	1	2	66,7%
13, 13	0	0	2	0	66.7%
15, 15	1	1	2	1	66.7%
17, 17	2	2	2	2	100.0%
19, 19	1	0	1	1	66.7%
21, 21	1	1	1	1	100.0%
23, 23	2	2	2	2	100.0%
25, 25	1	0	1	2	33.3%
27, 27	2	2	2	2	100.0%
29, 29	1	0	1	1	66.7%
31, 31	2	1	2	3	33.3%
33, 33	1	1	1	1	100.0%
35, 35	1	0	1	2	33.3%
37, 37	2	2	2	2	100.0%
39, 39	0	0	1	0	66.7%
41, 41	1	1	1	1	100.0%
43, 43	1	1	1	2	66.7%
47, 47	1	1	1	2	66.7%
49, 49	2	1	2	3	33.3%
51, 51	3	2	3	3	66.7%
53, 53	2	1	2	2	66.7%
55, 55	2	2	2	3	66.7%
Overall		60.9%	78.3%	65.2%	68.1%

Figure 4.1 Agreement among teachers — rating the engagement value of a student's story

The concept of reliability based on agreement of ratings can be used to design and test assessment instruments, as well as to evaluate assessment results. One feature of Robert Pavlica's high school science research program was periodic presentations by students of their research in progress. The criteria that were developed to evaluate critical elements of public presentations of research are displayed in **Figure 4.2**. Each criterion can be assigned one of three possible ratings:

0: Expectation Not Met

1: Expectation Met

2: Expectation Exceeded

The instructor chose to have an "expectation exceeded" level in order to encourage excellence and creativity. A wide variety of dispositions and skills are targeted in this assessment activity. Some of these criteria may be capabilities that can be applied productively in other educational venues and in situations outside of formal schooling (i.e., core capabilities). The basis of ratings was the observation of a presentation made to peers, and ratings were entered via desktop computers. (Each student had access to a separate computer.) Today, ratings can easily be entered via mobile devices as well. The presenter and teacher entered ratings and the option was available for visitors to the class to enter ratings as well. Students would be presented with these criteria as a prelude to preparing their presentations. They would also be forewarned that they may well receive ratings of 0 on many of the criteria during the early part of the course because the class has had no prior experience with the activity or the rating instrument.

0 1 2

◯ ◯ ◯ *i* Materials are ready and well organized

◯ ◯ ◯ *i* The presenter clearly introduces the topic

◯ ◯ ◯ *i* The research literature is effectively reviewed

◯ ◯ ◯ *i* The review of the literature is logically presented

◯ ◯ ◯ *i* The hypothesis is clearly stated

◯ ◯ ◯ *i* The presenter varies his/her inflection

◯ ◯ ◯ *i* The presenter is familiar and at ease with the topic

◯ ◯ ◯ *i* The presenter uses an appropriate level of language

◯ ◯ ◯ *i* The presenter pronounces words correctly

◯ ◯ ◯ *i* The presenter uses words correctly

◯ ◯ ◯ *i* The presenter maintains eye contact with the audience

◯ ◯ ◯ *i* The presenter maintains good posture

◯ ◯ ◯ *i* The presenter repeats questions and comments

◯ ◯ ◯ *i* Graphs, tables, and charts are properly titled and numbered

◯ ◯ ◯ *i* Data is presented so it is easily understood

◯ ◯ ◯ *i* Status of the hypothesis is clearly indicated

◯ ◯ ◯ *i* The presenter manages time well

◯ ◯ ◯ *i* The presenter closes the presentation effectively

Comments:

[   ]

(Submit Ratings)

Figure 4.2 Form for rating student research presentations

When raters hover over the ⓘ in the rating form as shown in **Figure 4.3**, additional detail as to how to rate performance on a criterion is revealed. The teacher refers to these explanatory or descriptive rating guides to the levels of attainment as "rubrics."

The rating form becomes accessible once the student presentation has been completed. This is to protect the presenter from the distracting effects of an audience attending to personal electronic devices. As soon as all ratings have been entered, summary reports are generated and appear projected on a screen for everyone to see.

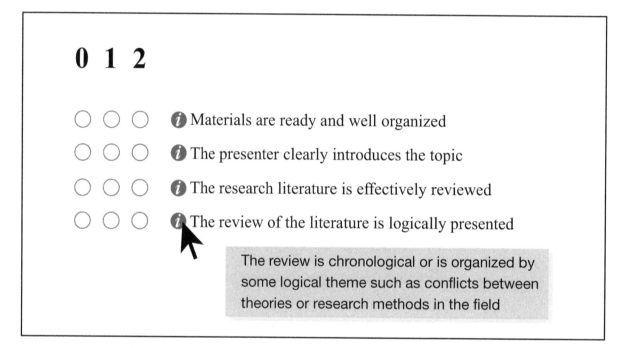

Figure 4.3 A pop-up gives more detail to help with rating the criterion
The review of the literature is logically presented

Figure 4.4 is a detailed report of student performance for an initial use of this rating instrument with a class. Imagine this analysis projected on a screen before the whole class. Each column contains the ratings made by a single individual. The three sets of results now to be presented are based on a typical sequence of rating events over the course of a school year.

Reports

The Interocular Traumatic Test of Significance

by Essie Dee

	Essie Dee	Teacher	Guest	± ± ± ± ± ± ± ± ± ±
Materials are ready and well organized	0	0	1	2 2 1 1 0 1 0 2 0
The presenter clearly introduces the topic	1	1	2	2 2 1 0 1 0 0 1 2 1
The research literature is effectively reviewed	0	0	0	2 2 1 1 0 1 0 2 0
The review of the literature is logically presented			1	2 2 0 1 0 1 0 2 0
The hypothesis is clearly stated	0	0	1	1 1 1 0 1 0 2 0
The presenter varies his/her inflection	0	0	0	1 1 1 1 0 0 1 0 2 0
The presenter is familiar and at ease with the topic	0	1	1	2 2 1 1 1 0 1 2 0
The presenter uses an appropriate level of language	0	0	1	2 1 1 0 1 0 1 0
The presenter pronounces words correctly	0	1	1	1 1 0 1 0 0 1 0
The presenter uses words correctly	0	0	0	1 1 0 1 0 1 0 1 0
The presenter maintains eye contact with the audience	0	0	0	1 0 1 0 0 0 0 1 0
The presenter maintains good posture	1	1	1	2 2 0 1 1 1 0 1 2 1
The presenter repeats questions and comments	0	0	0	1 2 0 1 0 0 2 0
Graphs, tables, and charts are properly titled and numbered	0	0	0	1 1 0 0 0 1 0 1 0
Data is presented so it is easily understood	1	0	1	1 1 0 1 1 1 0 2 0
Status of the hypothesis is clearly indicated	0	0	1	1 1 0 1 1 0 2 0
The presenter manages time well	0	0	1	2 2 0 1 1 0 2 0
The presenter closes the presentation effectively	1	2	1	2 2 1 1 0 1 2 1

Figure 4.4 Rating a student presentation — initial use of the rating instrument

Raters' names are masked except for those of the teacher and the student who is making the presentation. The teacher can reveal the students' names (*Clarice*, in this case) by clicking on the active ± sign at the head of a column as shown in **Figure 4.5**. But this feature is never activated when the class is in session. It is reserved exclusively for one-to-one evaluation sessions between teacher and student where that student's responses are studied in light of the full pattern of class response. Targeted personal instruction can be delivered in these sessions. Students can offer their insights into the presentation and the rating processes, as well as review their own ratings in comparison with others. In this example, a guest teacher has been invited to attend the presentation and join in the rating process to test for reliability of ratings. The student presenter (*Essie Dee*, in this case) has rated her own presentation. Students can see how teachers and the presenter rated the presentation but not each other's ratings.

Reports

The Interocular Traumatic Test of Significance

by Essie Dee

	Essie Dee	Teacher	Guest	± ± ± ± ± ± ± ± ± ±
Materials are ready and well organized	0	0	1	2 2 1 1 0 1 0 2 0
The presenter clearly introduces the topic	1	1	2	2 2 0 1 0 0 1 2 1
The research literature is effectively reviewed	0	0	0	2 2 1 1 0 1 0 2 0
The review of the literature is logically presented	0	0	1	2 2 0 1 0 1 0 2 0

Clarice

Figure 4.5 The teacher can reveal the identity of student raters

The results, every single item of which is rich with information for the teacher, may seem something of a jumble to an outsider observing them for the first time. Additional information will help. **Figure 4.6** shows a tally of the same ratings shown in **Figure 4.4**. To grasp the meaning of these ratings to the teacher, it is necessary to distinguish ratings of 0 (expectation not met) on the one hand from ratings of 1 and 2 (expectation attained or exceeded) on the other. While the difference between a 1 and a 2 might be considered a subjective judgment, there should be no disagreement concerning whether the expectation was met at all. So, for a first look, the observer should ignore, as the teacher does, the difference between 1 and 2, and simply compare 0's with the combined non-0's — that is, with the combined 1's and 2's. A box has been drawn around the 1's and 2's to facilitate this distinction. Blanks indicate occasions when no rating was made on the criterion. The sought-for quality of information here is a high and low proportion of ratings on one or another side of the demarcation, i.e., between "expectation not met" and the two possible values that indicate that the expectation was met. High and low proportions of ratings indicate agreement between raters. For example, there is a relatively high level of agreement that the presenter *clearly introduced the topic, maintained good posture,* and *closed the presentation effectively, i.e.,* 10 (6+4) out of 11 or 91% of the raters agreed that the presentation was closed effectively. There is also relatively high agreement that the presenter did not *maintain eye contact with the audience* and did not *properly title graphs, tables, and charts.*

Why would students' ratings differ on these criteria? What does it mean if students' ratings do not agree with the teacher's? What are the possible reasons for disagreement? These are important questions that typically cannot be addressed objectively in classrooms but can be laid out in the open for inspection in this environment. Consider a few possibilities. Perhaps a rater is biased in some way, favoring or disfavoring the rating object (in this case, the presentation or the presenter). Perhaps a rater does not understand the expectations associated with the rating criterion. It may also be that the rating instructions for any given criterion are unclear or otherwise defective. These situations come to light in conversation when results are presented to the group immediately following the presentation. The meaning and desired qualities of judgments on the criteria become explicit objects of attention, instruction, and even dispute, providing prime instructional opportunities. Students tend to become quite engaged in these discussions. Questions of objectivity vs. subjectivity, bias, fairness, reliability, and validity enter into the discussion and indeed can become learning goals themselves in addition to the substance of the capabilities targeted by the criteria.

At this stage, the teacher is particularly concerned that some students have given ratings as high as 2 (expectation exceeded) in cases where in actuality the presenter did not fulfill the criterion at all. Let's consider specific performance on several of the criteria in **Figure 4.6** from the point of view of the teacher.

The presenter repeats questions and comments

The substance of this criterion stems from the fact that in many presentation situations members of an audience may not be able to hear (or grasp) questions posed by someone in the audience. To remedy this potential problem, the presenter is enjoined to repeat or restate the question. Agreement regarding whether this was demonstrated should have been very straightforward: the presenter either did or did not repeat questions from the audience. That disagreement has surfaced may indicate that the rating criterion is not understood, or that raters have been inattentive, or that ratings are biased in some way. Regarding bias, the teacher notices that it is certain students that are consistently, and seemingly indiscriminately, giving ratings of 2 to many or most of the criteria. The presenter, teacher, and guest agree that questions were not repeated. Why then should anyone have given a rating of 1 or 2? A classroom conversation, with a projected image of the original ratings (**Figure 4.3**) in view is used as a basis for re-instituting understanding of the criterion and addressing issues of inattentiveness and bias.

The hypothesis is clearly stated

Again, what might be expected to be a straightforward rating criterion has resulted in widespread disagreement that includes the guest. The teacher realizes that the desired qualities of performance have not been made sufficiently explicit on this criterion.

The presenter uses an appropriate level of language

Disagreement on this criterion is again widespread among students and has again occurred between the teacher and the guest rater. It is not clear to the students or the rater how to make a judgment on this criterion. Disagreement with the guest is particularly troubling to the teacher. The teacher decides to review and improve the additional detail feature.

Several raters have consistently given ratings substantially below or above those given by the teacher. When the teacher next meets with these students in a one-on-one session to evaluate their work, students will be presented with these discrepancies and asked to provide the reasons for their ratings. Any lack of clarity concerning the criteria can be addressed then, but also the students can be held accountable for their ratings thanks to this report feature. Students learn in this way to be attentive and accurate in their ratings of presentations. One student has left ratings on many criteria blank. Conversation with the teacher reveals that he does not assign ratings when he is unsure of the meaning of the criterion or whether it has been met.

Reports

The Interocular Traumatic Test of Significance

by Essie Dee

	0	**1**	**2**
Materials are ready and well organized	5	4	3
The presenter clearly introduces the topic	3	6	4
The research literature is effectively reviewed	6	3	3
The review of the literature is logically presented	6	3	3
The hypothesis is clearly stated	5	5	1
The presenter varies his/her inflection	7	5	1
The presenter is familiar and at ease with the topic	3	6	3
The presenter uses an appropriate level of language	5	5	1
The presenter pronounces words correctly	5	6	
The presenter uses words correctly	7	5	
The presenter maintains eye contact with the audience	9	3	
The presenter maintains good posture	2	8	3
The presenter repeats questions and comments	7	2	2
Graphs, tables, and charts are properly titled and numbered	8	4	
Data is presented so it is easily understood	4	7	1
Status of the hypothesis is clearly indicated	5	5	1
The presenter manages time well	5	3	3
The presenter closes the presentation effectively	1	6	4

Figure 4.6 Tally of ratings on initial student presentation

Figure 4.7 displays detailed student ratings of the student's second presentation of her research (ITTS II) conducted midway in the use of this assessment instrument. There is now much less disagreement concerning whether the criteria have been attained. Apparent bias is still evident in the ratings of several students. These will be addressed in one-on-one meetings, although the full class review of results provides an excellent opportunity to point out and discuss this aspect of the results.

Reports

ITTS II

by Essie Dee

	Guest	Teacher	Essie Dee	± ± ± ± ± ± ± ± ± ± ±
Materials are ready and well organized	1	1	0	2 0 2 1 2 0 1　1 1 2
The presenter clearly introduces the topic	1	2	1	2 1 2 1 0 1 1 0 0 1 2
The research literature is effectively reviewed	0	0	0	2 0 2 1 1 0 0　1 0 1
The review of the literature is logically presented	1	1	1	2 0 2 0 1 1 1　1 1 1
The hypothesis is clearly stated	1	1	1	1 0 1 1　1 0 1 1 0 1
The presenter varies his/her inflection	0	0	0	1 0 1 1 1 0 0 0 1 0 0
The presenter is familiar and at ease with the topic	1	1	0	2 0 2 1 1 0 1　0 1 1
The presenter uses an appropriate level of language	1	1	1	2 0 1 1 0　0 1 1 0 1
The presenter pronounces words correctly	0	2	0	1　1 0 1 0 1　　0 1
The presenter uses words correctly	1	1	0	1 0 1　1　0 0 1 0
The presenter maintains eye contact with the audience	0	0	0	1 0 0 1 0　0 1　0 1
The presenter maintains good posture	1	1	1	2 1 1 0 1 1 1 0 0 1 2
The presenter repeats questions and comments	0	0	0	1 0 2 0 1 0 0 0　0 2
Graphs, tables, and charts are properly titled and numbered	0	0	0	1 0 1 0 0 0 0　0 0 0
Data is presented so it is easily understood	1	1	1	1 0　0 1 1 0　1 0 1
Status of the hypothesis is clearly indicated	1	1	1	1 0 1 0 1 1 0　1 0 1
The presenter manages time well	1	0	0	0 0 1 1 0 0 1 0 0 0 0
The presenter closes the presentation effectively	1	2	1	1 1 2 1 1 1 2 1 0 1 2

Figure 4.7 Detailed ratings of Essie Dee's second presentation — midway in the course

The tally of the midway presentation ratings in **Figure 4.8** indicates progress regarding several of the criteria. The agreement patterns on four of the criteria bear some attention. One student still seems to have an inordinate number of 2 ratings. These will have to be addressed at the one-on-one evaluation meeting with the teacher — similarly for one student who seems to be giving systematically low ratings. The student who does not rate when he is unsure concerning the criterion or the evidence of its attainment is rating an increasing number of criteria. This student can be considered a *canary in a coal mine* regarding failures of clarity in the assessment instrument.

Graphs, tables, and charts are properly titled and numbered

Again the teacher, presenter, and guest agreed that there were no graphic supports in the presentation. Why did some students give ratings of 1 or 2? This is addressed with the entire class while looking at a projection of these results.

The hypothesis is clearly stated

Agreement is increasing here, suggesting that learning is occurring and that the rating rubric has become better defined.

The presenter uses an appropriate level of language

The teacher has clarified the rubric to improve reliability of ratings. It now reads: "Terms and concepts which may not be familiar to members of the audience have been explained." Agreement has improved but not sufficiently in the teacher's mind. Discussion reveals that it is not always clear when such explanation is needed. The teacher points out that what is critical in this criterion is not that all such instances be identified and remedied, but rather the presenter should be sensitive to keeping the audience's level of understanding in mind. The teacher, in concert with the students, comes up with the idea that one instance of such an explanation signals the student's sensitivity to the issue. A student suggests that more than one instance of such an explanation deserves a rating of 2. The teacher likes this because it makes the rating of 2, at least in this case, more objective. Moreover, it will support attentiveness to the substance and process of the presentations. Too many such explanations would both reduce the presenters available presentation time and likely steal time away from other important criteria, and so there is a balancing factor that would keep the student circumspect regarding trying to score points by giving many such explanations.

The presenter manages time well

A timekeeper announces how long the presentation took. In this case, only the guest and one student disagree. The guest (who might be different on different occasions) does not know that the expectation for this criterion is that the presentation must take no more than 9 minutes and that the student took almost 11 minutes. The student who gave a rating of 2 will be asked at the next one-to-one meeting to provide the reasons for his rating. One student suggests that a 2 should be reserved for students whose presentation falls precisely between 8 and 9 minutes. The group might then discuss how to implement this suggestion.

Reports

ITTS II

by Essie Dee

	0	1	2
Materials are ready and well organized	3	6	4
The presenter clearly introduces the topic	3	7	4
The research literature is effectively reviewed	7	4	2
The review of the literature is logically presented	2	9	2
The hypothesis is clearly stated	3	10	
The presenter varies his/her inflection	9	5	
The presenter is familiar and at ease with the topic	4	7	2
The presenter uses an appropriate level of language	4	8	1
The presenter pronounces words correctly	5	6	
The presenter uses words correctly	5	6	
The presenter maintains eye contact with the audience	8	4	
The presenter maintains good posture	3	9	2
The presenter repeats questions and comments	9	2	2
Graphs, tables, and charts are properly titled and numbered	11	2	
Data is presented so it is easily understood	4	8	
Status of the hypothesis is clearly indicated	4	9	
The presenter manages time well	10	4	
The presenter closes the presentation effectively	1	9	4

Figure 4.8 Tally of ratings on student presentation — midway in the course

Figure 4.9 displays ratings on a third presentation given by the same student. The class has now had a good deal of experience using the rating procedure.

Reports

ITTS III

by Essie Dee

	Guest	Teacher	Essie Dee	±	±	±	±	±	±	±	±	±	±	±
Materials are ready and well organized	2	1	1	2	0	2	1	2	1	1		1	1	2
The presenter clearly introduces the topic	1	2	1	2	1	2	1	0	1	1	1	0	1	2
The research literature is effectively reviewed	1	1	1	2	0	2	1	1	1	1		1	1	1
The review of the literature is logically presented	2	1	1	2	1	2	0	1	1	1		1	1	1
The hypothesis is clearly stated	1	1	1	1	1	2	1			1	1	1	1	1
The presenter varies his/her inflection	1	1	1	1	0	1	1	1	0	0	0	1	0	1
The presenter is familiar and at ease with the topic	1	1	1	2	0	2	1	1	1	1		1	1	1
The presenter uses an appropriate level of language	1	1	1	2	0	1	1	0		0	1	1	0	1
The presenter pronounces words correctly	0	1	1	1		1	0		0				0	1
The presenter uses words correctly	1	1	1	1	0	1		1		0				0
The presenter maintains eye contact with the audience	1	1	1	1	0	1	1	1	1	0	1		1	1
The presenter maintains good posture	2	2	1	2	1	1	1	1	1	1	1	1	1	2
The presenter repeats questions and comments	2	1	1	2	1	2	1	1	1	1	1	1	1	2
Graphs, tables, and charts are properly titled and numbered	2	1	1	2	0	1	1	1	0	1	1	1	1	2
Data is presented so it is easily understood	1	1	1	2	0	1	1	1	1	1		1	1	1
Status of the hypothesis is clearly indicated	1	1	1	1	1	1	0	1	1	0	1	1	1	1
The presenter manages time well	0	0	0	0	0	0	0	0	0	0	0	0	0	0
The presenter closes the presentation effectively	1	2	1	2	1	2	2	1	1	2	1	0	1	2

Figure 4.9 Ratings of student presentation — experienced users of the rating instrument

Discrepancies between 0 ratings on the one hand and combined 1 and 2 ratings on the other are now rare. Ratings in the 0 column of the tally shown in **Figure 4.10** are now generally either very high or low. Students' grasp of how to apply the criteria to make ratings has developed substantially. There is greater consistency among the ratings. The ratings have become more *reliable*. Overall results strongly support the conclusion that the presenter has advanced in attainment of many of the targeted capabilities.

Overly favorable ratings of this student's presentations seem to be under control. This is due both to increasing sophistication in making ratings but also because the presenter's capabilities are improving. Still several students seem to be giving systematically low scores to this student. Do they do so for other students' presentations as well? The study of consistency (reliability) provides opportunities to examine questions of this kind objectively.

A number of students have begun leaving blank those items which they are unsure of. This is helpful to the teacher but creates some ambiguity with respect to items that they may simply have neglected to rate. The teacher considers creating a "not sure" category. This would be another indication concerning which items require instruction, as opposed to improvement of the assessment instrument.

Reports

ITTS III

by Essie Dee

	0	1	2
Materials are ready and well organized	1	7	5
The presenter clearly introduces the topic	2	8	4
The research literature is effectively reviewed	1	10	2
The review of the literature is logically presented	1	9	3
The hypothesis is clearly stated		12	1
The presenter varies his/her inflection	5	9	
The presenter is familiar and at ease with the topic	1	10	2
The presenter uses an appropriate level of language	4	8	1
The presenter pronounces words correctly	4	5	
The presenter uses words correctly	3	6	
The presenter maintains eye contact with the audience	2	11	
The presenter maintains good posture		10	4
The presenter repeats questions and comments		11	3
Graphs, tables, and charts are properly titled and numbered	2	9	3
Data is presented so it is easily understood	1	11	1
Status of the hypothesis is clearly indicated	2	12	
The presenter manages time well	14		
The presenter closes the presentation effectively	1	7	6

Figure 4.10 Tally of ratings on a student presentation — experienced users of the rating instrument

By examining how a student has been rated, a teacher can see the degree to which both rater and presenter have attained each of these targeted skills and dispositions. The teacher can discriminate when a student has not yet attained the concept underlying the capability by studying how the student rates other students on that capability. For example, if a student consistently misses the target in identifying whether the status of *the hypothesis is clearly indicated* for different students then the teacher has evidence that the student is having trouble with that concept. The concept of reliability goes beyond being simply a technique for evaluating and improving the quality of an assessment activity. It can become a way to monitor student attainment of capabilities, to identify need for more instruction, or to change the direction of instruction. Reliability reports can themselves be used as a method of instruction related to the targeted capabilities. Thus curriculum, instruction, assessment, and evaluation can be seamlessly interwoven in an educational activity working at the level of practical learning goals. Moreover, evaluations of the results in these cases provide suggestions to the teacher for formative improvement of curriculum, assessment, and evaluation. The summative results can be used to inform future iterations of the course. Students themselves can become active in making decisions on all of the course features, including curriculum. When one of us taught the *Science Research in the High School* course, using the Pavlica model described here, alumni would visit the class, act as guest raters, and suggest which capabilities had been most valuable to them in their postsecondary careers.

Such analyses open the door to further considerations — are these the most appropriate learning goals for this course? Are they core capabilities? These are questions for all stakeholders in educational communities, as well as for those who teach and take this course.

Ratings on these presentations were never incorporated into the course grades of the students. Yet, teachers of this course found that students were highly motivated to improve their presentations and that their use of the rating instrument improved consistently over time.

Questions often arise concerning how validity and reliability are related. The relationship is actually quite straightforward. As has been demonstrated, indicators of reliability are one of the ways to tell whether an assessment is valid. Failure to achieve reliability of judgments or ratings is evidence that some feature of the assessment is not effective, is not accomplishing what it should, and, to that extent, lacking in validity.

Timeliness

Ideally, assessment results are available to teachers in near real time while instruction is still underway. Results that are not available until after the close of a unit of instruction may have summative value but are of no help to the students currently receiving instruction. When attention is centered on the challenge of helping students attain a set of targeted learning goals, a premium must be put on having assessment results available in time to plan the next educational event. The ideal then, the highest value, is attained when a teacher is able to immediately and productively incorporate information on how well targeted learning goals are being attained at any moment in time. Computer-aided instructional activities and clicker- and plicker-based feedback can become useful aids in attaining such value. The rating and analysis of student research presentations described above demonstrates assessment, instruction, and evaluation occurring in real-time settings. Practical teacher education focused on developing capabilities needed to design, apply, and refine assessment and evaluation builds a professional scaffolding that prepares teachers for in-the-moment instructional action that productively incorporates the most current knowledge of student attainment of learning goals.

Efficiency

Some may argue that efficiency is a consideration that is appropriate for commercial or scientific environments, but not so when working with human beings. Actually, efficiency is a prime humane consideration when it comes to educational activities and programs. Time is perhaps the most valuable and limited resource for teachers and students. From the point of view of a teacher working with classes of students, there is hardly ever enough time to do things the way the teacher would like to do them. The effective use of students' time is equally important. Efficiency is about using that limited time well. Assessment and evaluation, essential though they may be, are time consuming and always threaten to take time or resources away from educational events. Consider the time involved in realizing educational assessment and evaluation:

1. Designing the assessment instrument and appropriate analysis

2. Testing the assessment instrument to assure that it works as intended

3. Developing competence in administering the assessment instrument

4. Administering the assessment to students

5. Reviewing, analyzing, and presenting the results

6. Applying assessment results to evaluate educational activities

How can these steps be made most efficient to save teacher and student time? Design time can be reduced, as suggested earlier, by using appropriate measures that have already been developed by others. Here is where standardized assessment instruments can be of benefit. Using existing, valid, and reliable assessments of targeted learning goals can pay off in efficiency and quality.

But the time devoted to assessment design and construction can itself be beneficial. Opportunities for teachers to collaborate in building assessments for the learning goals in their curriculum can be a profound professional development activity. If constructed and presented properly, the resulting assessment instruments can become resources of value, not only to school colleagues, but to teachers in other schools as well. Collaboration in testing each other's assessment items can contribute to reducing the second cost in the outline presented above.

Whenever possible, assessment activities should be designed to simultaneously deliver instruction. An assessment instrument can itself be an activity for helping students to attain learning goals. **Cubes and Liquids**[21] (Doane, Rice, & Zachos, 2006) is an assessment activity that takes one-half hour to administer. Its administration is at the same time instruction — students are obtaining direct experience of the natural phenomena and of the scientific methods that are the target of its six learning goals.

In the high school science research course, the time students spent in presenting, rating, and reviewing each other's research is simultaneously instruction and assessment. Once designed and actualized, assessment need not take time away from instruction but can add value to instruction itself. Time spent on assessment and evaluation in that course is instructionally productive and the teacher need spend hardly any additional effort in carrying out, analyzing, and reporting assessment results.

Edumetrics vs. Psychometrics

For more than 100 years, the field of measurement in educational programs has been dominated by a theoretical and research paradigm known as *psychometrics*. The theoretical underpinnings of psychometrics were established for the purpose of discriminating between individuals based on their differences in performance, primarily on cognitive tasks. This became the basis for intelligence tests and tests for selecting entrance into educational, business, and military programs. As such, psychometrics from the start has not been focused on teaching and learning processes. The promulgation of psychometric theory and methods within educational institutions has led to bizarre practices such as scoring tests and giving grades *on a curve,* practices that run counter to productive educational practice. This problem was recognized decades ago by Ronald Carver, who proposed that we needed to develop a science of measurement relevant to strictly educational decision-making, a science that he proposed be referred to as *edumetrics* (Carver, 1974).

Recognition of the inappropriateness of much psychometric theory and practice to educational decision-making has recently become more widely recognized and the term "classroom metrics" has been coined to refer to the new theory and practice that must be developed (Benson, 2003). Unfortunately, though well motivated in putting the focus on information that can be useful at the scene of teaching and learning,

---

[21] *http://acase.org/educational-assessment/*

the term is too limiting. The classroom is a temporal instrument, which, although the dominant setting of educational programs for 200 years, is now feeling the strain of contemporary realities. Increasingly, education is being provided in both massive and intimate settings outside of classrooms. Even in school environments, project-based and internship-modeled educational offerings are going beyond the limitations of classrooms. Classrooms themselves begin to dissolve as a concept when students in a class are working separately on computers on different tasks towards different learning goals. There is no reason why classrooms need to have their own metrics. It would make their outcomes incomparable with other educational efforts directed to the same learning goals. Indeed, we would want to be able to compare classroom-based methods for facilitating attainment of targeted learning goals with other methods. To limit theory and practice for educational measurement to classroom settings would be to miss the opportunity to develop a generic approach to educational assessment and evaluation. The later is the approach that is needed, and can be appropriately designated by the term *edumetrics*.

Implications

At present, validity and reliability are being construed almost exclusively for instruments in which outcomes associated with diverse learning goals are aggregated. These methods can only serve non-educational purposes. Aggregations across distinct learning goals obliterate the information contained in their distinct components — the information that is needed to support teaching and learning. Future guidelines for educational assessment and evaluation, e.g., successors to guidelines such as the *Standards for Educational and Psychological Testing* (American Educational Research Association (AERA) et al., 2014), and standard reference works such as *Educational Measurement* (Brennan, 2006) must more definitively address the need for a purely educational assessment and evaluation distinct from the methods and practices associated with high-stakes, norm-referenced testing. The *Classroom Assessment Standards for PreK-12 Teachers* (Joint Committee on Standards for Educational Evaluation, 2015) takes a strong positive step forward in gearing up assessment and evaluation to usefulness at the level of educational events. The next necessary step forward must be to address the questions of validity and reliability at the level of practical learning goals and outcomes. Looking back at the example from the astrobiology course in which diverse learning outcomes were aggregated to obtain an overall picture of performance in the domain of *conditions of life* (See the section of Chapter III entitled *Is Aggregation Across Diverse Learning Goals Necessarily Inappropriate?*), it should be clear that attempting to establish the validity and reliability of the aggregated scores would be missing the point of educational usefulness of the information entirely.

It is said that what is tested is valued. The reverse of this must be considered as well. The most valued learning goals (e.g., core capabilities) are the best starting point for thinking and action in education and for determining what should be assessed.

Conventional wisdom also states that "not everything can be measured" and not every learning goal can be assessed. The notion that certain learning goals cannot be assessed is applied most often to the realm of dispositions. There are two things wrong with these points of view. First of all, it is unwise to decide ahead of time that something cannot be done. Then, although there is nothing inherently wrong with using numbers to characterize levels of attainment, it is critical to recognize that assessment, in essence, is not about assigning numbers to levels of student performance. Rather assessment is about finding evidence concerning how well learning goals are being attained. It is always possible to find evidence concerning the attainment of any learning goal. Indeed, it is the responsibility of all players and stakeholders in educational programs to be perpetually on the lookout for evidence of how well students are attaining learning goals. Creativity in imagining and developing assessments for the full range of concepts, skills, *and* dispositions is needed to become the basis of renewing educational assessment and evaluation.

Summary

The usefulness of assessment information depends on the validity, reliability, timeliness, and efficiency of assessment instruments and procedures.

Questions of validity and reliability are not just the domain of educational specialists, but enter into and can be adequately addressed within the very fabric of any teacher's daily work.

The practice of establishing the validity and reliability of educational assessment methods must itself have relevance for educational events. This requires that the problems of validity and reliability be addressed at the level of practical learning goals and outcomes. The scene of action where teaching and learning is taking place must become the center of the educational information enterprise. This is where validity and reliability can have an appropriate impact on quality, meaningfulness, and the dependability of inferences about what students have attained. The complex statistical analyses associated with current methods of establishing validity and reliability are distractions from the practical problems of providing education.

Assessments conducted at the end of a unit or course cannot serve educational purposes for the students presently receiving instruction. The usefulness of assessment outcome information is greatest when a teacher applies it in planning the very next steps in instruction. Assessment results that are not timely lose their educational usefulness.

Efficiency is critical because the time and resources available to teacher, learner, and the supporting community are limited and precious. An assessment activity that is educational — i.e., is intended to help students attain learning goals as well as to find out if learning goals have been attained — supports instructional efficiency. Assessment and evaluation that are embedded in instruction in this way do not take time away from instruction. They represent a high point of efficiency in educational programs.

CHAPTER V
How Information Failures Spawn Educational Disasters

What was actually learned and what was not? If we cannot answer these simple questions, we will not be able to adequately address any of the divisive educational problems of our time, or even most of the simpler ones. Accountability, merit pay, cheating, and the many other burning and seemingly impenetrable controversies can all be revisited productively in the light of the proper use of essential educational information. Instead of solving contemporary educational problems, high-stakes norm-referenced testing and grading are generating and exacerbating them. At the same time, some of the most maligned practices in contemporary education hold great promise for true educational reform.

Chapter V
How Information Failures Spawn
Educational Disasters

It's deja vu all over again.

Yogi Berra

In 1714, responding to over a century of naval inefficiencies and disasters, the British Parliament offered a prize of £20,000, the so-called "Queen Anne's Prize," to whomever could solve the problem of measuring longitude. Dava Sobel and William Andrewes relate how the efforts of the greatest minds of the British Royal Society directed to this problem were exhausted in vain and how John Harrison recognized that the solution required a *chronometer*, a device for precisely measuring time in the active environment of ocean travel (Sobel & Andrewes, 1998). Information derived from high-stakes, norm-referenced testing and grading has created more of a problem than a solution to the challenge of improving educational programs. Mauritz Johnson's discovery of the central role of intended learning outcomes in educational thinking and action laid the foundation for establishing the critical unit of educational information. Assessment of the attainment of learning outcomes aligned with *practical learning goals* provides the "chronometer" for educational decision-making — the information needed to navigate (i.e., to grasp and take efficient action) at the active scene of educational events.

What Happened to the Great 20th Century Educational Innovations?

The 20th century gave birth to remarkable ideas and innovations directed to the delivery of improved education. Consider the work of just a few of the educational giants of the early part of the century — John Dewey, Maria Montessori, and Rudolf Steiner, who presented their respective discoveries of evolutionary stages in children's learning and how to address these through instruction. Consider also the foundations for a science and technology of education that emerged in the second half of the century with the goal of bringing innovations to fruition for all — Benjamin Bloom's notion of *Mastery Learning,* William Spady's *Outcome-Based Education,* Mauritz Johnson's model, and the profound contributions to assessment of learning pioneered by Bärbel Inhelder and Jean Piaget. Yet, after a century of efforts towards "educational reform," the inspired visions and efforts of these and many other innovators have left barely a surface scratch on everyday practice in mainstream education. Only hints remain of these contributions in the current research literature, nothing of the inspiration and interest they once aroused and should still. Several generations of reformers, particularly since the 1960s in the United States, have each successively designed and executed massive programs of educational reform at great expenditure of effort and public resources, each of which has moved inexorably to decline, dismantling, and replacement by the next reform effort, with little to show in the way of accomplishment. For example, none has left even a simple legacy identifying that valued learning outcomes were attained in association with particular methods or programs. In the face of this cyclical onslaught of reform efforts, teachers and school officials have learned to shield themselves against successive reform initiatives, preparing for how to ride the current wave as painlessly as possible until it passes and they can get back to business as usual. Colossal initiatives are again and again launched and carried forward for a period of years, often in association with substantial collateral damage, until they slowly disintegrate. The very notion of educational reform itself has come under suspicion with prominent educational thinkers, suggesting that government initiated reform efforts of the last few decades in the United States have been driven by the agenda of undermining public education (Glass, 2008; Ravitch, 2010).

The Problem of Educational Reform

For a solid overview of contemporary educational reform movements in the United States, it is worth examining Jane David and Larry Cuban's extensive study of this phenomenon. Their survey takes into consideration the history and varieties of contemporary efforts directed to reforming educational systems in the U.S., including reorganizing schools and bringing about changes in teaching practices (David & Cuban, 2010). Charter schools, test-based accountability, increased time in school, attempts to impact systems, institutions, and instructional practice, and the hopes and ultimate problems associated with each are considered in the light of social, political, and economic forces, as well as purely educational issues addressed by two seasoned educators.

At present, schools in the United States are in the midst of what is often called *standards based-educational reform*. Students, teachers, schools, and even states are to be held accountable for student performance with regard to educational *standards*. But what are educational *standards?* They are nothing other than learning goals. One might imagine then that progress has finally been made by putting learning goals at the heart of a reform effort, that what we have been proposing in *Knowing the Learner* has finally worked its way into the educational mainstream. Sadly, it is quite the reverse. When Bruce MacLaury introduces Diane Ravitch's classic work *National Standards in American Education* (Ravitch, 1995), he asks "What should American students know and how does society know they have learned it?" In this concise statement, we find two of the three fundamental educational questions as they relate to public policy — "What are the goals for learning?" and "How do we know that the goals are being attained?" But something goes terribly awry in producing the answers to these questions. Attempts are made to take massive social action related to these questions before they have been answered in a way that can serve as a productive basis for action. In the end, attention to individual standards is completely lost and high-stakes, norm-referenced measures are adopted almost universally to make teachers, programs, and institutions socially accountable. This is in spite of the fact that these HSNR methods are devoid of meaning and usefulness at the level of educational events, at the scene where teaching and learning takes place, the place where reform efforts could actually have their desired beneficial effects.

The Information Gap in Educational Reform

To grasp the depth of the educational reform problem, it is necessary to consider the situation from an information perspective. This allows a dramatic picture to emerge. Were all the technical, administrative, and social problems called to our attention by David and Cuban to be solved, there still would not be an adequate solution to the strictly educational problems that need to be addressed. This is because there is one fundamental educational problem that, if not solved, will remain a persistent obstacle to resolving all of the others, a problem that will interfere with all social and political efforts to reform educational activities and programs. This is that virtually all of the efforts at educational reform at all levels, from the student to the state, are working with the wrong information!

The instruments of accountability in the current round of reform efforts have increasingly become student performance on high-stakes, norm-referenced tests. Reformers have almost exclusively tried to exercise accountability based on the HSNR paradigm, with instruments of information, decision-making, and action that are not themselves accountable — that is, they are not sensitive to the practical need to know how well students have attained distinct learning goals. This is why HSNR-based testing and evaluation are not capable of supporting educational activities and inevitably work to the detriment of educational efforts. For example, raising levels of proficiency or expectation on test performance, and creating items at varying levels of difficulty in order to more efficiently rank and scale student performance simply tells nothing about what has been or needs to be attained and how to support attainment. HSNR test reports are generally not aligned to the day-to-day curriculum nor do they provide information that can be used to constructively inform educational activities. They leave an information chasm between the directors of reform and the scene where learning is to take place. They replace the higher goals for learning, the higher capabilities that teachers wish to devote their attention to with the need to defer to institutional expedience. This distraction from the educational business at hand decreases effectiveness because critical time and attention is stolen from educational efforts and events. Additionally, the disconnect between the teacher's perception of educational need and the pressure to perform well on an insensitive instrument acts as an inhibition to creativity, innovation, and the possibility of meaningful reform itself (Nichols & Berliner, 2007). Future attempts at innovation and reform will similarly be crushed in the path of HSNR-based evaluation because it cannot either discern or produce educational value. Teachers, schools administrators, state educational agencies — all abandon their duties and best judgment concerning what students most need to learn and how to help them learn it and end up scrambling about trying to figure out how to prepare students to do well on HSNR tests. But these tests, produced at gargantuan expense and investment of resources, can do no more than declare some students, teachers, or programs better or worse than others in some respect. Attempts to make useful policy decisions based on conventional test results at any level persistently show themselves fruitless. Systems of policy, decision-making, and action based on HSNR test scores can only make things worse because they direct attention, effort, and resources away from a program's main purposes. They do provide huge windfall profits for the commercial testing industry and for private organizations that prepare students to do well on HSNR tests, but that is certainly not the end to which the resources intended for public education should be directed.

As this book is nearing completion, in the United States, the National Science Foundation, The Institute of Educational Sciences (the research wing of the U.S. Department of Education), and the American Educational Research Association are teaming up to set common evidence standards for educational research in relation to Common Core standards. The Common Core standards are a way to operationalize what we have called *core capabilities* in a research- and evidence-based context to meet the demands of 21st century life and culture (Kendall, 2011).[22] But the initiative is in disarray, in part because it was swallowed up by the HSNR testing and evaluation paradigm. As a result, the Common Core initiative runs the risk of meeting the same fate as all the other reform efforts that have placed their eggs in the HSNR basket. New York State has adopted an initiative known as *Annual Professional Performance Review* (APPR)[23] that has many of the features we have been advocating here, including ground-level assessment and evaluation conducted by teachers working with practical learning goals and aligned assessment instruments. However, the potential benefits of the approach have been completely overwhelmed and subverted by making the system subservient to HSNR test results. A new approach is needed.

Educational Reform in Essence (True Educational Reform)

But what is educational reform really? It is decision and action based on evaluation results directed to changing some feature of an educational program or activity that needs to be improved. Looking purely at educational activities, what may need to

---

[22] *http://www.corestandards.org/the-standards*

[23] *https://www.engageny.org/resource/appr-3012-d*

change may be the curriculum — it may be the assessment, it may be instruction, it may even be the evaluation itself. Evaluation may also reveal the need to reform some non-educational feature of the programs (e.g., the need to provide scholarships to worthy students who do not have the resources to educate themselves). In its essence, reform is simply the response to evaluation, action directed to increasing the value of educational activities and programs. Every course, every lesson, every educational event properly becomes the scene of reform and innovation. Productive reform could be brought about for each teacher, school, district, and state. But the resources, and particularly the information critical to reform, would have to be available and used strictly for the purpose of helping students to attain learning goals (e.g., professional education related to targeted core capabilities).

More Burning Questions Related to Information Misuse

For true reform to take effect and be sustained, it must take place on the basis of knowing the learner, the learning goal, and the cultural context of the program. Let us consider some of the more controversial/problematic issues in the field of education today in the light of this perspective.

The Problems of Accountability, Teacher Evaluation, and Merit Pay

In a collective social enterprise such as publicly supported education, all participants — teachers, students, parents, supervisors and administrators, government officials, and providers of educational resources — should be accountable for their actions. *But what forms precisely should that accountability take for each of these stakeholders?* The public mind today is focused primarily on teacher accountability. At the time of the writing of this book, teachers are being held accountable for the performance of their students on high-stakes, norm-referenced tests. Hiding in the shadows behind this practice is the assumption that we can know the effects of teaching on students' test performance. Hiding more deeply is an assumption of causality — the assumption that teachers' actions or lack thereof are a cause of the level of student performance on these tests. It seems straightforward that there should be some relationship between teachers' actions and students' attainment. The whole educational enterprise is founded on this assumption. But what can we soundly infer about the actual relationship?

A large number of factors would have to be considered to build any such causal equation. To begin with, there are the numerous human attributes that need to be taken into account (including student intention, motivation, interest, previous learning, learning habits, and cultural factors such as level of competency in language in which test is administered, and socioeconomic well-being). These constitute competing explanations for level of success on assessments and tests. Some of these (e.g., *interest*) might themselves be considered worthy goals for learning, often more worthy than stated course content itself. Many teachers take on the challenge of developing these as capabilities, but, of course, HSNR tests neither measure nor take these capabilities into account. Consequently, the exclusive use of such instruments reduces the evaluation of teaching and learning to improperly defined content and format.

Then there are questions of the effects of poverty/wealth, cultural enrichment/deprivation, and sense of security/insecurity on student performance. Might such effects have as great or greater an influence on student performance than the experience of spending a period of time with a particular teacher? What proportion of these factors can a teacher reasonably be held accountable for? How can we tease out the effects of such factors?

We must consider the attributes of teachers as well. How long have they been teaching? What preparation do they have? What resources do they have available? What support are they obtaining from colleagues and from the school community as a whole? These would all have to be entered into the equation. Valid and reliable assessment and research instruments would need to be developed for each of these attributes and then applied and integrated into interpretations of students' performance. The Institute of Educational Sciences sets a premium on funding research that employs randomized control trials (RCT) as a basis for inferences of causality in educational settings. But RCT studies struggle persistently, and unsuccessfully, with the problem of *over-determination* — that is, situations "...where a number of factors are present, any one of which could have produced the same result that is being attributed to the intervention" (Cook, Scriven, Coryn, & Evergreen, 2010).

In actuality, *no* school has the resources to conduct studies to permit the inference of causality. It turns out that the attempt to tease out these attributes in order to establish causal effects of a teacher's action is not a feasible enterprise. In fact, it constitutes a monstrous pseudoscience. Therefore, on what basis do states and schools make the inference that the teacher or the teacher's method is responsible for students' performance on a test? The answer is on *no sound rational or empirical basis at all!* There is no way that research to establish cause (as a feature of instruction) and effect (as the performance on a HSNR test) could be carried out other than in highly restricted artificial educational settings. The cost would be too great, the conditions could not be met, and the inferences could be easily challenged on the basis of the argument that the results could have been attained without the method of instruction used (Klees, 2016).

But all such attempts at relating student performance to teacher performance neglect the most fundamental questions of all. Do the assessment instruments provide information on the attainment of targeted learning outcomes, those to which teachers' efforts should be directed and for which teachers might truly feel accountable? Do any of the assessments used in educational programs measure what is most important (e.g., core capabilities)? Are they accurate and dependable measures of the learning goals that constitute the program's aim? The reader should not be surprised at this point to realize that, for the most part, none of these conditions are met. Again, we are led to the sad realization that those who engage in these virtually omnipresent processes of establishing teacher accountability are resting on the cultural belief that HSNR tests are the best available way to measure the value of instruction. Once the pseudo-scientific attribution of causality is discarded, the entire justification for attempts by school districts, states, and federal agencies to manipulate educational programs based on HSNR tests collapses, its lack of foundation evident and its potential for harm exposed. Any thought of basing teacher evaluation or teacher accountability on such instruments should be immediately and roundly dismissed. Naturally, any proposals for merit pay based on HSNR test results must quickly be allowed to fall by the wayside as well.

The strongest basis for sound educational decision-making that we have at present is the considered judgments of seasoned, dedicated teachers based on their knowledge of their students and these teachers' facility in working with targeted learning goals. Is it wise to lose these treasures in deference to policies and authorities operating in ignorance at a hyper distance from the teaching learning process?

Systematic educational assessment and community-based educational evaluation such as we have proposed in the preceding chapters give a sound basis for accountability in the context of professional development and program improvement. The most productive next step that we can take at present towards teacher accountability is a purely educational one. It is part of the realization of teacher as learner. It can be accomplished in the context of helping teachers learn how to use assessment information to help students attain the practical learning outcomes for their curriculum. As education is a social enterprise, teachers who cannot learn to help students attain the targeted learning goals that make up the curriculum must inevitably chose to leave of their own volition in the face of public reports of assessment results. Accountability of teachers and students (indeed, all facets of educational programs from the student to the state) are critical. But, first, the instruments and procedures of accountability must themselves be made accountable. They must show their efficacy in supporting educational activities and events.

Is High-Stakes, Norm-Referenced (HSNR) Testing Needed at All?

For many — and particularly for those who have never experienced anything different in educational institutions — this question may never have been posed or seriously considered. Many consider HSNR tests and grades to be a necessary evil, performing a critical function that, unfortunately, produces collateral damage. The literature on harmful effects associated with HSNR testing and associated grading practices is extensive (Abeles & Rubenstein, 2015; Hoffman, 1962; Kohn, 2000;

Koretz, 2008; Popham, 1999; Ravitch, 2010). This in itself presents sufficient cause for concern, but, more to the point, the starting assumption that HSNR tests play a critical role is itself bankrupt. This recognition dawns when it becomes evident that results from HSNR tests do not supply information that can be used to support teaching and learning and, as a result, are used almost exclusively for non-educational applications. This is the reason why deleterious side effects associated with HSNR testing and conventional grading practices are inevitable. But what are the imagined critical functions? Susan Brookhart details these functions clearly and thoroughly in her book *How to Make Decisions with Different Kinds of Student Assessment Data* (Brookhart, 2016), where high-stakes, norm-referenced testing is given a significant role. This role includes accountability, grading, and small- and large-scale evaluation in support of educational programs and events. But recall that we have argued for the necessity of divorcing grading from assessment in Chapter I and have outlined the universal applicability of practical learning outcome information as the most salient information for all of the other functions in Chapter III. There is simply no educational purpose for which HSNR tests are currently thought to be useful that can't be served more simply, more directly, and more effectively through reports on the attainment of learning outcomes aligned to practical learning goals. HSNR testing and conventional grading practices are not only deleterious but actually not educationally useful at all. If this is so, then there is no reason why high-stakes, norm-referenced testing should continue to be used in educational programs. One of the raging questions in the field of education today in the United States is how much testing is appropriate and whether there is too much testing. President Barack Obama himself took a stand on this question.[24, 25] But there is no need to appeal to authority. Based on the analysis presented thus far in *Knowing the Learner*, the question can be answered definitively: If it is *HSNR testing, it is too much testing!*

But our presentation so far leads to another remarkable conclusion — there is *not enough assessment!* Henry Roediger and Mark McDaniel's research indicates that frequent quizzes can be a powerful tool for strengthening and deepening learning (McDaniel, Agarwal, Huelser, McDermott, & Roediger III, 2011; Roediger III, Agarwal, McDaniel, & McDermott, 2011), and Stuart Yeh has documented strong motivational effects on teachers and students of frequent assessment that reveals student progress (Yeh, 2006). But this is not HSNR testing and grading; it is assessment carried out to support the attainment of targeted learning goals. Assessment can itself, if properly designed, serve as instruction, and there is no reason why assessment cannot be interesting, engaging, motivating, and provide fulfilling experiences for students. Peter Brown takes the trouble to point out that what Roediger and McDaniel and their colleagues are talking about and call "low-stakes quizzing and self-testing" is an

---

[24] *http://boston.com/news/nation/articles/2011/03/28/obama_says_standardized_tests_often_punitive/*

[25] *http://dianeravitch.net/2015/10/24/obama-administration-admits-there-is-too-much-testing/*

activity devoted exclusively to supporting intended learning (Brown et al., 2014, p. 69). If it is entirely instructional and effective, there cannot be too much assessment! A lesson to draw from Roediger et al's research is not only that we should assess more, but that the more challenging the assessment, the deeper and more permanent the learning. Appropriate assessment not only gives an indication of the degree to which learning has occurred; it can consolidate learning itself!

Standardization Is Not the Enemy!

The reader may have noticed that we have been careful to direct our criticism to *high-stakes, norm-referenced testing* and not to *standardized testing*. The term *standardized testing* has become quite the bogeyman for many critics of educational reform (Kohn, 2000). To understand why this is so, we need to examine the history of standardized testing over the past century. Looking back to the beginning of the 20th century, we find the work of Alfred Binet, who created the first "intelligence" tests for the purpose of discriminating, among those considered to be mentally retarded, individuals who were to be considered educable from those to be considered non-educable. These tests were initially a one-on-one clinical instrument that evolved over the years into "paper and pencil" tests of intelligence and then tests of logical mathematical and linguistic capabilities, such as those standardized tests widely used in college admissions processes. Common to all these tests was the idea of developing cutoff scores to discriminate what were considered to be distinct levels of native or learned capabilities. The science of *psychometrics* developed in part to assure the quality of these tests. Along with psychometrics came assumptions that neither fit nor served well the purposes of education. One was the assumption that human capabilities fall into patterns that can be modeled by a normal curve — that is, that the performances levels of students on a test will fall into dependable proportions of the curve, e.g., 2% of performances will appear at a certain score above and below the average score. Conventional tests are actually constructed so that this wish for "normality" will be satisfied. Such test design allows one to set a cutoff and say that students above a certain level will pass, or be admitted to some privilege, or receive a certain grade. This has resulted in the practice of scoring tests in educational settings "on a curve." You may have experienced this in your career as a student or a teacher. A certain percentage of students are to receive A, B, C, D, or F ("F" is for failure) as their score on the test or for their grade in a course.

What if all students perform poorly on a test? Following the grading on a curve approach, their performance measures would still be lined up in order and assigned corresponding scores (e.g., A+ to the top 2%, A to the next 8%, B+ to the next 12%, etc. all the way down), with slight manipulations of scores when there are many duplicates of the same score.

What if all students performed very well on the test, i.e., attained almost all of the items on the test? Their performance measures would still be lined up and assigned corresponding scores (A+ to the top 2%, A to the next 8%, B+ to the next 12%, etc. all the way down) with slight manipulations of scores when there are many duplicates of the same score.

But what if all students failed every item on the test or passed every item on the test? Typically this has been considered a failure of the test. But is that really the case? It may simply mean that students had either attained all of the learning goals being assessed or none of them. These two meaningful and important pieces of information that are essential to educational considerations are anathema to the norm-referencing model of design and analysis. In any case, whatever the distribution of scores across the range of performance — whatever the shape of the curve — the reduction of information on performance to a single value (the test score or grade) makes the information unusable for educational considerations — that is, for helping anyone attain learning goals. In scoring on a curve, the teacher ceases to be a servant of education and becomes a servant of ideology, a servant of institutional practices that rank and scale people indifferent to educational intentions and ends.

But the true purpose of standardization is something quite distinct from scaling and comparing people. The purpose of standardizing an assessment instrument is to assure the accuracy and dependability of the results obtained. For example, **Cubes and Liquids**[26] produces accurate and dependable results concerning student attainment because there are precise rules for administering the activity that elicit student performance and precise rules for judging the level of attainment of the learning goals. Moreover, pains have been taken to assure that the content of the assessments is aligned with the nature of the learning goals and the capabilities that they represent. In this sense, **Cubes and Liquids**, which is designed to help teachers plan instruction — and for other purely educational purposes — can be considered a *standardized* assessment instrument.

Is *Teaching to the Test* Necessarily Bad?

The process of designing assessments itself can make a valuable contribution to the conduct and quality of instruction. When we begin to consider what evidence will satisfy us that a learning goal has been attained, we also begin to envision, in a practical way, the ends towards which instruction is leading. But does this not lead us into the highly deprecated practice of *teaching to the test?* Perhaps, but first we should consider why teaching to the test has such a bad name. The reason, generally, can be traced back to high-stakes, norm-referenced testing and grading. If the grade that will be assigned on a test is going to influence a student's status and opportunities now or in the future, many learners will turn their primary attention to what they need to do

---

[26] *http://acase.org/educational-assessment/*

to maximize their test scores. This is a disruptive distraction from the subject matter of instruction, and, in fact, often spoils the joy of the learning process for both teacher and student. When the assessment is a high-stakes, norm-referenced test that does not bear a one-to-one relationship to what is being taught, we have multiplied the distraction and the deleterious side effects. In such a situation, the teacher has also become co-opted into abandoning the original goals of instruction in order to see to it that the score against which she and the student will be evaluated is maximized. This is one of the reasons why HSNR instruments and practices cannot be used effectively to evaluate and improve instruction — because they actually lead teacher and student away from the true targets of instruction to try to maximize performance on tests that may be far different from what students are supposed to be learning. But what if assessments produced true and accurate evidence of the capabilities that we wish to develop in our students? What if we used the resulting information to support intended learning? Why would we not want to teach in a way that would lead to clear demonstration of the desired capabilities? Of course, neither teaching nor assessment are the aims of education, but rather the means of helping the learner to attain valued capabilities that may be inferred from learning outcomes.

The Problem of Cheating in Educational Programs

Cheating is a common practice in educational institutions at all levels. Students cheat teachers; teachers cheat the systems in which they are working; school systems cheat the states to which they are held accountable. People try to cheat systems because they feel that the systems do not serve their interests or advantage. But it seems contradictory and shameful that educational systems would not be serving the interests and advantage of those who participate in and are supposed to be served by them. It takes little reflection to recognize that much of the cheating that takes place in educational institutions is attributable to the dominance of the high-stakes, norm-referenced testing and grading practices. If assessment was structured exclusively around the aim of helping learners to attain valued learning outcomes and if evaluation was carried out strictly to support teaching and learning in order to inform both teachers and students, there would be dramatically less reason to cheat. Moreover, if there was an understanding that assessment results were to be used strictly to improve instruction, there would be much less reason, perhaps little reason at all, for the massive secrecy associated with efforts to keep the contents of assessments secure. Valid and reliable assessments could be developed and shared by institutions and teachers, and used as a basis for building cumulative knowledge and practice around targeted learning goals. Concern that teachers or schools are misrepresenting assessment findings could be investigated by strategically comparing samples of teacher assessment ratings with those made by an independent rater. This would identify teachers who need professional development in their assessment practices, but, more importantly, could begin to do away with the vast and expensive apparatus of test security and secrecy.

Standards-Based Grading

One of the current initiatives associated with the standards-based educational reform movement is referred to as *standards-based grading*. This movement advocates an assignment of grades to students based on how well they perform on tests associated with the educational standards, the learning goals officially adopted by states, e.g., those associated with the *Common Core State Standards Initiative* (Vatterott, 2015). After all, standards have been set for student attainment — why not give students grades based on those standards, and why not evaluate teachers based on the attainment of their students on those standards? This prospect seems self-evident and so is achieving widespread adoption. The underlying assumption, however, is empty of value. Cannot the failure of a student to attain a learning goal be attributed as easily to failure on the part of the teacher to deliver appropriate instruction as to a failure on the part of the student? If a student does everything that a teacher requires and still does not attain a learning goal, is failure the student's or the teacher's responsibility? The basis for answering such questions is not a simple one. We hope that the presentation on *accomplishment-based grading* in Chapter I has demonstrated sufficiently that, on the one hand standards-based grading is not an innovative idea, and that ultimately it is likely to be non-informative as well as corrosive to educational productivity. The standards-based grading initiative reveals that many educational practitioners and policymakers have still not recognized the haphazard and destructive impacts that grading based on assessment information can have on the conduct of educational activities, and on the relationship between teacher and student.

Implications

It is necessary to avoid repeating the history of errors associated with using high-stakes, norm-referenced tests as an instrument of educational reform. Moreover, key features of the problems associated with accountability, cheating, and teaching to the test can be remedied by replacing HSNR testing and grading with truly educational assessment and evaluation.

Summary

Accountability is not the purpose of educational programs.

Evaluation is not the purpose of educational programs.

Even instruction or teaching is not the purpose of educational programs.

The purpose of education programs is developing human capabilities.

Research and evaluation questions directed to provide information useful at the scene of the educational event require information concerning how well valued human capabilities, targeted by practical learning goals, are being achieved. Historic reform efforts have failed, and current educational reform movements will not be able to move forward effectively because they are not based on this critical type of information — they are basing their inferences, decisions, and actions on the wrong information.

The essential information on which to base educational planning and action, i.e., how well valued learning outcomes have been attained, is missing from most educational reform efforts. Turning to performance on high-stakes, norm-referenced tests as the criterion of educational success generates a monolithic force in the face of which hardly a whisper, leave alone a lasting impression of innovation, can survive in the educational mainstream. Certainly, much discipline and creativity has been directed to preparing learners to do well on HSNR tests, but this cannot be considered a valued outcome of general education or a worthy expenditure of educational resources.

Unquestionably, all those who take part in educational enterprises under public auspices are accountable for their actions. But first those who seek to impose accountability on education and make educational institutions the servants of their mission must show that their methods and actions are themselves accountable, that they are demonstrably at the service of the educational enterprise. To do so, assessment and evaluation must work with outcome information aligned to practical learning goals and assure that their actions are directly supportive of and do not distract from educational practice.

Educational reform is the responsibility of every player and stakeholder in educational programs and institutions. It is the application of evaluation to improve — that is, to increase the value of, curriculum, assessment, instruction, and evaluation itself. Evaluation associated with the purely educational use of learning outcome information is the surest basis for practical and constructive reform.

CHAPTER VI
Renewing Educational Assessment, Evaluation, and Research

The improvement of educational practice depends on the disciplines of assessment, evaluation, and research. Yet, in spite of a century of expansion and the expenditure of vast resources, these disciplines have had negligible impact on daily educational practice. What lies behind this seeming contradiction?

Chapter VI
Renewing Educational Assessment, Evaluation, and Research

...not the kind of assessment used to give grades or to satisfy the accountability demands of an external authority, but rather the kind of assessment that can be used as part of instruction to support and enhance learning. On this topic, I am especially interested in engaging the very large number of educational researchers who participate, in one way or another, in teacher education. The transformation of assessment practices cannot be accomplished in separate tests and measurement courses, but rather should be a central concern in teaching methods courses. (Shepard, 2000, p. 1)

The Method of Stipulating Definitions

Knowing the Learner is filled with many terms familiar to the field of education — e.g., *assessment, evaluation,* and *curriculum.* The apparent obviousness of their meaning can be misleading. We have followed Mauritz Johnson's practice of stipulating definitions in situations where there is no agreement on the use of terms or when a concept is needed for which there is no precise equivalent or appropriate term in use. This situation is clearly the case with the terms *assessment* and *evaluation* in education. Grasping the presentation that follows requires abiding by our stipulated definitions. Definitions of additional terms that are critical to the present discussion such as *curriculum* and *instruction* can be found in the glossary. While our use of terms is not inconsistent with common use, the purposes to which they have been directed and the precise nature of the definitions given here requires attention and fidelity while working with the present text. There is no expectation that readers will continue to apply these definitions outside of the context of this book. We believe, however, that the clarity that ensues from the distinctions made here will provide sound foundations for productive approaches to many educational issues. The term *educational activities* itself has been defined operationally here and used with precision throughout the book. The present chapter highlights the negative consequences of not having clear and precise concepts and definitions for the essential educational activities.

Assessment *Is Not* Evaluation

There is a good deal of variation in how the terms *assessment* and *evaluation* are defined and applied in the educational literature. *The Standards for Educational and Psychological Testing* (American Educational Research Association (AERA) et al., 2014) gives a very broad definition to the term *assessment.* The definition encompasses a wide range of variegated tests and inventories that goes far beyond the assessment of learning. We find it productive to have a term that refers exclusively to obtaining, analyzing, and presenting information on how well discrete learning goals are being attained. This is the term *educational assessment*. The term *educational evaluation,* by contrast, will refer exclusively to using information to make decisions directed to increasing the value of educational activities. The terms assessment and evaluation as used in *Knowing the Learner* almost always refer to *educational assessment* and *educational evaluation.*

Evaluation is the application of information for the purpose of improving educational activities. Information on the attainment of learning outcomes (assessment results) is usually at the center of evaluation, but assessment information emerges in a context rich with information from many sources regarding environmental features of educational programs, including school and classroom organization, institutional procedures, teacher performance, and instruction. Additionally, there is information about students as individuals drawn from sources other than assessment. All of these types of information can enter into the process of evaluation. Evaluation, necessarily, must be carried out iteratively and, as often as is reasonable, without distracting from or interfering with ongoing educational activities.

The term *evaluation* is often used with regard to students. We do not speak of evaluating students but rather of assessment of student learning and evaluation of student accomplishments (e.g., the worthy accomplishments discussed in Chapter I). It makes sense to speak of judgment and decision-making directed to increasing the value of student accomplishments or of educational programs and activities, but it does not make sense, in our minds, to speak of increasing the value of students. Therefore we do not use the term *evaluate* in reference to students. This distinction is directed to remedying some of the dehumanizing effects associated with conventional testing and grading practices and their misuse in educational evaluation and decision-making.

The Redemption of Evaluation

Why does the thought of being evaluated strike fear into the participants in educational programs at every level — student, teacher, administrator? Why would we want fear to be a feature of educational programs? Can we heal the wound of evaluation? Can we reverse fear of evaluation to achieve interest in evaluation, appreciation of evaluation, desire for evaluation?

Over the last decade, inspired by indications given by Michael Scriven[27] and Robert Pruzek[28], the authors of the present book have been working with a renewed vision of the nature and practice of *educational evaluation* as a process associated with increasing the

---

[27] *http://MichaelScriven.info*

[28] *http://RMPruzek.com*

value of programs and activities and not primarily of judgments as to their worthiness. Except in the case of self-education, evaluation is a social activity. It works most effectively when it includes not only teachers and supervisors but learners, their parents, and experts from within and beyond the community. The more perspectives that can reasonably be brought into the evaluation process, the greater will be the resources available for program improvement. One of Mauritz Johnson's last projects was a *Citizen's Guide to Assessing School Programs*, an attempt to capitalize on such resources.[29] The possibility of bringing together diverse individuals from the immediate and larger community in support of an educational program leads naturally to considering the act of evaluation as a basis for building educational community, as well as for programmatic improvement. In essence, evaluation consists of efforts to increase the value of educational activities through constructive use of information about each of the fundamental educational activities — including evaluation itself! The central challenge for educational assessment is to provide teachers and learners with the information needed to support creative action at the scene of educational events. The challenge for evaluation is to continually lubricate educational activities so that they effectively support the realization of intended learning outcomes. The criterion against which all that we present here should be evaluated is how well it can support effective action at the scene of the educational event. Evaluation must have direct and immediate payoff, in the moment, in real educational settings.

Formative vs. Summative Evaluation

Michael Scriven made a lasting contribution to the field of evaluation by distinguishing between *formative evaluation* and *summative evaluation* (Scriven, 1967). This distinction continues to be productive when applied to educational programs. Formative evaluation takes place when educational activities are still underway. Formative evaluation provides the possibility of making changes to improve those living activities. Formative evaluation can *inform* educational decision-making at the scene of the event and, thereby, lead to *forming* or *reforming* the program's features and activities. Formative evaluation must be dynamic, timely, and efficient. Summative evaluation takes place when an educational program or activity has been completed. Summative evaluation provides the opportunity to make changes and improvements only in future programs and only in the education of future groups of learners because the program has come to an end.

Historically, most evaluation in educational programs has been summative — a learner completed a lesson, unit, or course, was tested, and received a grade. Interim test information might have been used formatively, but rarely was. It is now generally recognized that a fruitful change will come about for education with increases in the

---

[29] *http://acase.org/mjohnson/citizensguide.pdf*

formative application of student outcome information to improve instruction and other features of programs. As a result, the term *formative assessment* has come into use. However, the theories and practices associated with the use of this term have resulted in a number of serious problems.

The Problems with "Formative Assessment"

The idea underlying what people are calling *formative assessment* is simple and important, indeed necessary. It is the idea that assessment information can be used to improve educational activities, i.e., to have a constructive formative influence over these activities. But the meaning of the term *formative assessment* was never clearly established and its application has resulted in great waste and confusion in the field of education for over two decades. It should be self-evident that information on learning outcomes can be applied productively to improve educational programs and activities. Why then have immense amounts of money been spent conducting research to demonstrate that this can be the case? The scale and immensity of resources invested in such research itself reveals that something is seriously wrong with thinking on the subject. Profound errors are associated with the *formative assessment* enterprise and its literature.

Many of the problems originate in the *conflation* (or inappropriate combination) of what should be distinct ideas. The most common is the failure to distinguish assessment from evaluation — that is, the failure to distinguish the production of information (assessment) from the application of that information for planning and decision-making (evaluation). Clearly these are two distinct activities, but the term *formative assessment* in itself muddles them. Assessment results are best thought of simply as information. There is nothing necessarily formative or summative about information. It is the application of that information (i.e., evaluation) that can be formative or summative. Educational thinkers and researchers who are careful and precise in their thinking avoid such conflation. For example, James Pellegrino speaks in terms of "...assessments to assist learning or the formative use of assessment" (Pellegrino, 2014, p. 233). As Jeffrey Smith puts it, "Formative evaluation is the underlying purpose of this assessment and the relationship of the assessment approach to relevant instructional goals is the primary quality concern" (Smith, 2003).

The conflation of assessment with evaluation is only the beginning of the problem. Going back at least as far as the appearance of an influential paper by D. Royce Sadler (Sadler, 1989), giving *feedback* to students based on assessment results has been treated as a characteristic feature of *formative assessment*. But giving feedback to students is neither assessment nor evaluation; it is *instruction*. Recent compilations of formative assessment theory and practice make evident that this conflation is almost omnipresent (Andrade & Cizek, 2010). Granted, theoreticians, researchers, and practitioners using the concept of *formative assessment* have noble intentions. They are trying, as we are here, to distinguish the use of assessment information, which supports teaching and learning from those practices of ranking and accountability that do not do so (Black, Harrison, Lee, Marshall, & Wiliam, 2004, p. 10). Unfortunately, many critical distinctions and actions are lost in the single-minded focus on feedback. First of all, feedback is not the only formative use that can be made of assessment results. A teacher might well choose not to provide feedback to students on their performance but rather to alter instruction in some other way. Feedback is not a necessary action to follow assessment results — it may not even be a wise one. Philippe Perrenoud points out the extremely constraining effects that fixation on feedback has on educational thinking and action (Perrenoud, 1998). Mechanically giving feedback on student attainment may constitute a distraction from an instructional event that could incorporate assessment results in a more creative manner.

The almost-omnipresent conflation of assessment with instruction in so-called *formative assessment* is particularly problematic in that instruction is only one of the features of educational activities that may need to be changed or improved after examining assessment results. The best decision to make after examining assessment results might be to change the curriculum (e.g., the students may not be ready for the targeted learning goals or may be way beyond them). Or the best decision based on assessment results may be to change the assessment itself (e.g., the method of assessing is not providing the information about student attainment that is needed). Instruction is not necessarily what needs to be changed, and feedback does not necessarily need to be given.

The conflation problem persists further. Susan Brookhart has noted that some of the leading advocates of *formative assessment* believe that this activity should include student awareness and application of the idea of learning goals and the development of learning goals as a part of students' learning strategies (Brookhart, 2003). But that then threatens to conflate assessment with curriculum development — that is, the specification of learning goals. It is a wonderful idea to have students develop the capability to set their own learning goals, but why call that assessment? The conflation of curriculum and assessment once again removes instructional discretion from the teacher just as the conflation of assessment did with instruction. Some teachers may have reason to bring consideration of learning goals explicitly into an instructional presentation; others, quite rightfully, depending on what they are trying to accomplish, may not make the learning goals manifest at all. Particularly with younger learners, an emphasis on learning goals might well constitute a distraction or even a burden in students' relationship to the instruction underway. This is not to suggest in any way that students cannot be an integral part of curriculum development, simply that we should not make the mistake of speaking of curriculum development (i.e., the setting of learning goals) as if it is *assessment*. Assessment and evaluation can certainly become instruments of engagement in learning processes and collaboration in problem-solving, but that should be a matter of instructional discretion.

Is "Formative Assessment" Taking Place at All?

The problem goes beyond conflation and raises concerns that put the entire *formative assessment* enterprise into question. Imagine that clarity could be achieved by undoing all of the conflations described above. The way should then be clear to make use of assessment results formatively, i.e., to provide information that can be used to improve educational activities in progress. But there still remains one problem so severe that it reveals that the *formative assessment* enterprise lacks coherence with its basic intentions. There is much talk in the field of assessment these days concerning the appropriate level of granularity of information needed for formative use of assessment information at the level of instruction. Coarse-grained assessment information is typically considered to be associated with summative evaluation and high-stakes, norm-referenced testing (HSNR). Fine-grained assessment information is associated with formative use (Cizek, 2010). Rightfully, the notion of coarse- vs. fine-grained information refers to the need for assessment information to be at a level of specificity appropriate for formative purposes at the scene of teaching and learning. We have addressed this earlier through the concept of the *critical level of specificity.* What is not generally recognized is that so-called coarse-grained assessment information is considered to be coarse-grained largely because it consists of aggregated outcomes of diverse learning goals. Such aggregates do not have the information needed for educational planning and decision-making at the level of instruction and so cannot be used formatively. The conventional notion of granularity addresses the need for specificity of assessment information; it does not address the necessity for the information to be aligned with distinct learning goals so that the information may be used productively for the formative purposes imagined. The need for assessment results to be aligned to distinct learning goals if they are to be used formatively is virtually absent in the *formative assessment* literature. This leads to the, perhaps shocking, conclusion that not only is *formative assessment* a confusing term, but that there is serious question of how much, if any, formative use of assessment information can be taking place at all in the situations described in the literature.

It should be no surprise then, as Randy Elliot Bennett has demonstrated, that the absence of clarity and precision that characterize the *formative assessment* enterprise have resulted in an inability of its proponents to develop a coherent foundation for theory or a useful paradigm for practice and, consequently, a failure to obtain dependable research results (Bennett, 2011). The conflations described above play a substantial role in that failure. Curriculum, assessment, instruction, and evaluation have been unthinkingly intermingled and wide-scale confusion and lack of effectiveness have been the consequences.

"Classroom Assessment" as a Substitute for "Formative Assessment"

Activity has been underway to alleviate some of these problems by turning attention away from the term *formative assessment* and substituting the term *classroom assessment* (McMillan, 2013). The classroom assessment enterprise is also driven by the worthy goal of having assessment and evaluation practices contribute to teaching and learning as opposed to the non-educational practices and effects associated with high-stakes, norm-referenced testing and grading. But this again turns out to be an unfortunate choice of terms. True, much of what goes on in mainstream educational programs goes on in classrooms, and certainly assessment and evaluation practices need to be developed that will be of the greatest value in those venues. But do we really want to restrict education to classrooms? Educational programs are already offered in widening types of environments: podcasts, MOOCs, interactive online courses, outdoor education, informal education, living history, homeschooling, etc. Concepts and techniques of assessment and evaluation are needed that are applicable to educational improvement in all settings and conditions — not just for the classroom a venue that may increasingly cease to be the ideal setting for education as the new century progresses. Clearly appropriate assessment and evaluation must be provided to the millions of teachers and students currently working in classrooms, but the classroom must not be deified as *the* instrument of education. Furthermore, the *classroom assessment* movement has also not come to grips with the necessity of working with distinct learning goals at the *critical level of specificity* as a basis for formative use of assessment information, nor has it made progress in distinguishing assessment from evaluation.

Middle school students on a wintry day. The Sun and Shadows Assessment Activity.

Educational Assessment *Is* Educational Research

Assessment of attainment of learning goals may provide the most important information for educational evaluation, but it cannot be the only information on which to base decisions. Educational decision makers at every level, from the student to the state, need to incorporate information about the characteristics of learners, teachers, and learning environments into their thinking and action. Towards this end, additional research is required, research that will enrich interpretations and actions based on learning outcomes. But note that in this light, assessment (obtaining, analyzing, and presenting information on how well learning goals have been attained) *is,* by its very nature, educational research! The teacher, in conducting assessment and making decisions on how to increase the value of the educational services provided is a researcher and evaluator! Research and evaluation are often distinguished as activities that have generic vs. local applications, respectively. In the concluding portion of *Knowing the Learner,* we will suggest a way in which information from local programs can serve a generic function, that it can be of value to educational programs in general as well as for the specific programs in which it is collected. We have already indicated that the reverse is true, that information from international assessments can and should be used in planning, evaluating, and improving local educational programs. We have also already discussed the fundamental educational evaluation questions. Purely and simply, they are: How can curriculum, assessment, and instruction (and planning, implementation, and evaluation themselves) be improved? But what are the fundamental questions for educational research? That is, what is the most critical information needed to plan, evaluate, and improve educational programs and activities directed to the attainment of targeted learning outcomes? We propose they are the following:

1. What are the most critical human capabilities to be developed in any particular time and conditions?

2. How is the attainment of these capabilities most efficiently and accurately assessed?

3. What are the best ways to help learners attain targeted learning goals?

4. What are the critical features of teacher competence?

5. How can these critical features best be assessed?

6. How can these features best be developed?

7. What are the obstacles to answering the above questions?

8. How can the obstacles be overcome?

9. How can cumulative knowledge be built in education, such as that which characterizes the other arts and sciences? (Johnson, 1985)

This is a grand reiteration and interplay of the fundamental educational activities. We argue that the answers to questions 4-9 must follow competent responses to questions 1-3. All of these questions must be answered at the level of learning outcomes aligned with practical learning goals. Teacher competence itself will ultimately need to be defined by setting practical learning goals for educator competence and identifying the relationship between their attainment and success in facilitating the attainment of practical learning outcomes by students.

In every case, programs of educational research and development in order to realize the above research prospectus require the following:

1. Identifying learning goals for core capabilities

2. Developing assessments of core capabilities by diverse means (multiple and diverse means of assessing the same learning goal help to establish the validity of assessment items)

3. Identifying and studying the critical factors associated with efficient attainment of these capabilities. These factors are not different from the ones educational researchers have been concerned with over the last century. These include:

   a. Instructional methods (including features of the educational environment)

   b. Teacher characteristics

   c. Student characteristics

4. Studying the effects of the attainment of capabilities on the attainment of other capabilities (confirming core capabilities empirically)

Professional educational researchers and developers can in this way provide teachers, supervisors, planners, and decision makers with the information they need to plan, carry out, and evaluate the progress of educational activities. The approach just presented suggests important possibilities for focusing in on the most important issues, both because it is founded on core capabilities, but also because it can address the complexity that characterizes students, teachers, educational settings, and educational events through a foundation in practical learning goals.

Another fruitful direction for educational research would be to highlight the ways in which concepts, skills, and dispositions interact. This line of research, too, would need to be carried out at the level of practical learning outcomes. At present, learning outcomes are considered primarily as indicators of the endpoints of educational activities. Increasingly, we must think of them formatively, i.e., as prerequisites for planning learning activities, and, to do so, we must work at the level of practical learning outcomes.

All of these sources of information provide the raw and refined resources that permit educational evaluation to carry out its business of increasing the value of educational programs and activities.

The State of Educational Research — Limitations of Current Meta-Analyses

There is hardly a more informative way to overview the goals and accomplishments of educational research to date than to examine the results of meta-analyses. Meta-analysis of educational research uses statistical technology applied to summarize previous research findings. It is based on suggestions offered by Gene V. Glass (Glass, McGraw, & Smith, 1981). One of the most significant contributions to the field of education in the last few decades is John Hattie's *Visible Learning* (Hattie, 2009), which is a summary of meta-analyses in the field of education. It is perhaps the most notable effort towards synthesizing educational findings in the service of building cumulative knowledge. Incorporating results from hundreds of pieces of research, Hattie takes the reader on a grand tour of the instructional issues and theories of our time directed to the question: How do we best facilitate the attainment of learning goals? Hattie presents a lively picture of what could be happening most productively at the scene of the educational event:

> *The art in any synthesis is the overall message, and the simple adage underlying most of the syntheses in this book is "visible teaching and learning". Visible teaching and learning occurs when learning is the explicit goal, when it is appropriately challenging, when the teacher and the student both (in their various ways) seek to ascertain whether and to what degree the challenging goal is attained, when there is deliberate practice aimed at attaining mastery of the goal, when there is feedback given and sought, and when there are active, passionate, and engaging people (teacher, student, peers, and so on) participating in the act of learning.*

(Hattie, 2009, p. 22)

But there is a crucial distinction that must be made between Hattie's endeavor and what we are presenting in *Knowing the Learner*. Here, too, we are placing the research and evaluation functions at the service of supporting educational activities and events. But we believe that, to do so, information must be available in terms of distinct learning outcomes aligned to practical learning goals. This is the information about the learner that teachers need to make decisions and take action. All other information concerning educational programs and activities becomes educationally useful only when it is related to practical learning outcomes. Educational research also needs to be working with distinct learning goals at the critical level of specificity.

So far meta-analysis results are not based on such information; therefore, they are not useful at the scene of the educational event where specific learning goals, students, and cultural contexts are in play. *Visible Learning* is an inspiring realization of how educational research findings could be summarized, but, before such methods can be put to the service of educational events, they must be carried out again at the level of practical learning goals where the effects of the factors of interest can be concretely and productively summarized and acted upon. The field of educational research struggles daily to attribute causality beyond a reasonable doubt to methods of instruction but does not use as its building blocks something that could be established "beyond reasonable doubt" (i.e., how well individual learning goals have been attained).

Implications

Based on a purely educational agenda and founded on purely educational information, an age of truly educational research can begin. Much like educational reform efforts, educational research has been unable to have a substantial impact because it has not been based on practical learning outcomes for core capabilities. Consequently, it has not been able to focus attention on reaching conclusions that are relevant to working at the scene of educational events.

Summary

The point of grasping the stipulated definitions presented in *Knowing the Learner* is not to make these definitions official. It is to learn to become precise in educational communication and action. Clarity concerning several long-standing issues can be obtained by making sharp and productive distinctions between the activities of educational assessment and those of educational evaluation. This distinction sheds light on the nature and potential of educational research. As is the case with educational assessment, educational evaluation and research have not been progressing sufficiently because our institutions are working with the wrong information and misusing the information that they have.

All current notions of what is instructionally viable and productive need to be revisited and re-imagined in the light of the notion of practical learning goals. For example, can we really say that there are "best teaching practices" in general without knowing the specific learning goals? Can we say that a 150-person lecture hall or a million-person MOOC platform is less effective than an inquiry method for supporting the attainment of a learning goal without knowing the learning goal and who the student is? Is a single instructional method equally ideal for developing *the disposition to make persistent efforts* as it is for developing *the skill of distinguishing impressionism from expressionism in painting?* Is it always good practice to present learning goals to students before instruction? Is it better to answer a student's question directly or to have the student find the answer through her own effort? By now, we hope it is evident that the answers to all of these questions depend on knowing the learning goal, the learner, and the cultural context, and that their relationship needs to be examined empirically at the scene of educational events.

CHAPTER VII
Teacher as Learner, Learner as Teacher: Education in the 21st Century

Information can become more timely, more meaningful, and more relevant in support to every day educational practice. Its application can become more efficient and more humane. A creative approach to educational information can be directed to deepening the relationship between teacher and learner. We invite our readers to join us in conversation and action to build educational community on the basis of a new approach to educational information.

Chapter VII
Teacher as Learner, Learner as Teacher: Education in the 21ˢᵗ Century

With the skilled eye of a pediatrician and a trust in her insight, Maria Montessori was able to observe how disadvantaged learners went about educating themselves:

> *What was the wonder due to? No one could state it clearly. But it conquered me for ever, because it penetrated my heart as a new light. One day I looked at them with eyes which saw them differently, and I asked myself: 'Who are you? Are you the same children you were before?' And I said within myself: 'Perhaps you are those children of whom it was said that they would come to save humanity. If so, I shall follow you.' Since then, I am she who tries to grasp their message and to follow them. And in order to follow them, I changed my whole life. I was nearly 40. I had in front of me a doctor's career and a professorship at the University. But I left all, because I felt compelled to follow [these children], and to find others who could follow them, for I saw that in them lay the secret of the soul.[30]*

Can we now, strengthened by our burgeoning abilities to know the learner through a new approach to educational information, begin to take decisive steps to improve the outcomes of educational activities and programs?

What follows are presentations on our current initiatives and ideas that we feel are worthy of pursuit in the present century. Each is accompanied by a pathway to development or participation.

---

[30] *https://montessori.org.au/history/sanlorenzo.htm*

Teacher as Learner

New models for adult and professional education are needed. They must be competency based, efficiently targeted to participant needs and respectful of participants' individualities. One of the authors' current initiatives directed to these needs is an online course in educational assessment and evaluation. We call it **EA&E Online**.[31] We refer to it affectionately as an *IMOC — an Intimate, Monitored, Online Course* — to distinguish it from the popular *MOOCs — Massive, Open, Online Courses*. The "I" of IMOC might well stand for *interactive*, since interactivity between instructor and participant is one of the primary characteristics of the course. The intimacy has to do with a special feature of EA&E — this is that participants come to know each other's educational work and personal proclivities in great detail as the course progresses.

As with any educational program, teacher education and professional development must begin by identifying critical (core) learning goals and applying valid assessments of their attainment. EA&E is organized around the *12 Fundamental Learning Goals* that we consider central to competent thinking and action in educational assessment and evaluation, but also for educational planning, implementation, and improvement in general (see Appendix A). Think of the course as a practical laboratory of teacher-initiated projects, projects that the course participants manage in their own home educational environment. Course participants design and bring to life three sets of *Educational Activities* — one devoted to a concept, another regarding a skill, and the third directed to a disposition. Participants design assessments and instruction for these activities. They iteratively carry out the assessments, evaluate their reliability and validity, and produce an Evaluation Report at three separate points in time for each Educational Activity. Design, conduct, and evaluation of the Educational Activities are carried out through a process of participant peer review under the supervision of the instructor, using an instrument known as the *Indicators of Quality for Educational Activities* (IQEA) (see Appendix B). Participants' work strives to meet a central criterion for sound educational research since the activities and products are designed to be replicable and applicable to programs beyond the local ones in which they are realized and tested. Much of the work is asynchronous, allowing participants to work in accordance with their personal schedules. Periodic "real-time" meetings are held (e.g., chats and audio/video conference calls) where live conversations between participants and instructor are organized around both technical and substantive questions.

---

[31] *http://EducationalRenewal.org/forum/courses/*

111

EA&E is an online version of *Knowing the Learner* brought into the realm of practice via the actual building, testing, and evaluation of educational activities. Ample opportunities to obtain evidence of how well participants have attained the 12 Learning Goals emerge in the process of carrying out and evaluating their own and fellow participants' Evaluation Reports in the context of a peer review environment. Participants are able at any point during the course to access evaluations of their Educational Activities and to view the instructors' ratings of their levels of attainment on the 12 Learning Goals. As the course progresses, participants begin to facilitate each other's attainment of the 12 Learning Goals. Thus participants are both teachers and learners, givers and receivers of professional development in assessment and evaluation.

Are these 12 Learning Goals truly the fundamental learning goals for grasping educational assessment and evaluation that we hold them to be? Is our assertion warranted that these are *core professional capabilities* for educators? These are empirical questions, of course, ones that we are engaged in answering and which we invite other researchers to investigate. The questions are addressed experientially in each iteration of the course, in ongoing conversation with each new set of participants, and with course completers (whom we refer to as *EA&E Fellows*). These same 12 Learning Goals underlie the content of this book. In *Knowing the Learner,* we have addressed the concepts underlying these learning goals with examples from our own past experience. EA&E course participants work directly to develop the capabilities in the context of their own educational programs. The heart of EA&E is participants' own valued learning goals for their students.

Learner as Teacher

In many online classes, learners are physically isolated from one another and from the teacher. They engage in the class by consuming the resources offered by the teacher and, occasionally, responding to posts from others through hierarchical discussion threads. Such learning environments present both opportunities and challenges. On one hand, learners who might be reluctant to jump into a face-to-face classroom discussion have the opportunity to marshal their thoughts. Learners at a distance are more insulated from comparing their own performance to that of others. Such isolation, however, demands that the teacher be creative in inviting learners to reflect on their own progress with respect to intended learning goals. Further, teachers need to invite learners to situate their learning within the context of their own life experiences. This both grounds their learning in examples with which they are already familiar and ensures that they are fully engaged to make learning meaningful for themselves.

In our teaching experience, it has been a vital component of face-to-face, online, and hybrid classes that learners understand that they are largely responsible for constructing their learning experience based on their prior knowledge and

112

experiences grounded in the new concepts, skills, and dispositions targeted by the course. In this way, learners themselves are the producers of novel applications of the class material they're encountering for the first time. Learners teach teachers new ways of applying and contextualizing academic ideas, enriching both learners' and teachers' understanding of the material.

In a set of project-based learning (PBL) (Markham, 2011) courses offered at a large, U.S. research university, one of the authors and a collaborating professor brought together graduate, pre-service school library media specialists and undergraduate web development students to design, develop, and deploy web-based learning materials for use in high-needs, urban K-12 classrooms. Enrolled university students worked with K-12 classroom teachers and in-service school library media specialists to identify learning goals for the project, design web-based instructional content, and assess K-12 students' degree of attainment of the targeted learning goals (Doane & Stefl-Mabry, 2009; Stefl-Mabry & Doane, 2008, 2014).

Note the authentic, layered nature of this experience — for university students, there were a set of learning goals, instructional plans, and assessments of attainment related to their university classwork. Part of those instructional plans involved engaging the university students themselves as real-world educators to develop a set of learning goals, instructional plans, and assessments of attainment related to K-12 students' classwork. At each step, we took pains to ensure that our students understood this intentional educational pattern and were actively engaged in metacognitively reflecting on the experience.

Over the course of nearly a decade teaching these courses together, we had the opportunity to teach undergraduate web-development students who, having become interested in education through the experience, enrolled in our graduate programs and then participated as graduate, pre-service school library media specialists. Many of our graduate students went on to become in-service school library media specialists and returned to work with our new cohorts of graduate and undergraduate students, thus completing the virtuous cycle. Contact: Joette Stefl-Mabry at jstefl-mabry@albany.edu

Learner as Evaluator

Invitations to Learn is Carol Ann Tomlinson's inspired identification of features of educational programs that may have an effect on program success (Tomlinson, 2002). What makes *Invitations to Learn* so interesting, information-wise, is that it is based on student judgments. Under five categories — *Affirmation, Contribution, Purpose, Power,* and *Challenge* — students express their perceptions of critical features of the educational programs in which they find themselves. For example, the *Challenge* category addresses students' perceptions of whether the following conditions are true in their educational environment:

- The work here complements my ability.

- The work stretches me.
- I work hard in this classroom.
- When I work hard, I generally succeed.
- I am accountable for my own growth, and I contribute to the growth of others.
- I accomplish things here that I didn't believe were possible.

The full set of *Invitations to Learn* is presented in Appendix E.

Imagine students using these criteria to rate features of the educational program in which they participate. Individual ratings would certainly be strongly tinged with subjective experience, and as such could grant insight concerning the student. But what if significant numbers of students in a program consistently gave the same response to any of these items? What if reliable indications of the program's qualities began to emerge? Such ratings could provide indicators of what might need to be improved, or of a teacher or school that is successfully developing a climate to support learning of valued student outcomes. Many of these criteria are themselves dispositions, qualities that could be productively developed in individuals, as well as features of educational programs to be evaluated. Some of these dispositions might even turn out to be core capabilities. Progress of students, teachers, and programs could be monitored through such surveys. Sessions in which ratings are reviewed, such as those described earlier for the *Science Research in the High School* course, would provide a forum for group considerations of the *Invitations*. In one such session, one of the authors was pleasantly surprised to find that many students reacted to a presentation of survey results by expressing the desire to improve themselves and their environment with respect to these qualities.

Why are evaluations based on such information not an integral part of how educational programs operate? Might not *Invitations to Learn* and other such indicators be part of an instrument of vital signs for educational programs? Is there a reason why we would not want such information? Might it be because we are afraid to have our programs evaluated? Might it be that we would find a dramatic need for change? Initially ratings of this sort might have to be made anonymously for fear of retribution or manipulation, but as an institution becomes increasingly based on trust, on mutual support in the relations between participants at all levels, ratings could be made more transparently.

A productive research program could also be developed based on Tomlinson's *Invitations to Learn*. Research questions such as the following might be posed:

- What is the relationship between *Invitations to Learn* ratings and success in attaining various learning goals?
- Could transformation of school climate be monitored via progress on various *Invitations to Learn* criteria?

Evaluations such as the Research Alliance for New York City Schools' study of the relationship between measures of school climate, student attainment, and teacher turnover[32] could be productively based on *Invitations to Learn* ratings. The U.S. Department of Education's School Climate Surveys (EDSCLS),[33] developed by the American Institutes for Research[34] is a survey instrument that has been directed to a similar purpose. This is very much the kind of support that governments can be giving to educational programs. John Hattie, in his more recent work, has seen the virtue of having a self-evaluation tool for teachers focusing on dispositions such as *I have high expectations for all, I welcome error, I know the power of peers* (Hattie, 2012). Readers interested in following up on these indications, please contact Paul Zachos at paz@acase.org

---

[32] *http://steinhardt.nyu.edu/research_alliance/publications/schools_as_organizations*

[33] *https://safesupportivelearning.ed.gov/edscls*

[34] *http://www.air.org*

A Great Reversal

Education reform could be designed and realized from the ground up instead of from the top down. Practicing teachers can become the primary producers and consumers of assessment information rather than simply its instruments and recipients. Teachers can develop, validate, and share curriculum, assessment activities, and instructional methods. Teachers can become the active agents in evaluation and practical education research. In her book, *Teaching Problems and the Problems of Teaching,* Magdalene Lampert demonstrates an effective teacher-based research model working at the level of practical learning goals and incorporating ongoing evaluation and improvement of curriculum, assessment, and instruction (Lampert, 2001). Lampert's work, moreover, is imbued with the notion of core capabilities and is directed to dispositions such as *intellectual courage, intellectual honesty,* and *wise restraint,* as well as to concepts and skills.

Teachers can become lead players in "research-practice partnerships," working in conjunction with government agencies and university and private research institutes, bringing the theme and substance of actual educational events to the forefront of this work:

Rather than developing studies that address gaps in existing theory or research, they focus on problems of practice — key dilemmas and challenges that practitioners face.

(Coburn & Penuel, 2016, p. 49)

The same is true for the development of policy. Universities serve as examples of how policies can be set by members of the faculty who are actively teaching. Waldorf schools are conceptually organized so that administrators execute organizational policies and educational priorities that are set by teacher councils (Gladstone, 1997).

To effect such a dramatic reversal of roles and responsibility, two major changes would have to be instituted:

1. Teachers who wish to engage in the full breadth of educational activity, including overall policy and decision-making, would need to be allotted the time and resources to carry out this work.

2. Teachers who wish to engage in such work must be able to develop and demonstrate competence in the fundamentals of their profession just as doctors, lawyers, and engineers do.

Teachers actively engaged in general education settings are able, at present, to take only the smallest of steps in such a direction on their own. One way to enhance their options and powers of action in these arenas, without unnecessary centralization and creation of hierarchies of authority, would be through the formation and support of *education networks.* Such networks would be independent of institutions, ideologies, and special interests. They would not be directed to serving the personal interests of teachers but rather the needs of learners and the cause of quality education in general. These networks could be the instrument by means of which educators could interact with stakeholders in the field of education (e.g., schools, states, academic and scientific communities and businesses, and interested members of the general public). The networks would be devoted to identifying educational needs and problems, with developing, refining, and sharing resources needed to address the problems. The resources could be methods and products associated with curriculum, assessment, instruction, and evaluation. The resources could also include research and policy recommendations related to effective realization of the fundamental educational activities or addressing educational issues. Membership would be open to anyone who is actively teaching or supporting teaching at any level. The idea is that educational events are the most central scene of productive action and that much is to be gained both locally and in general from the perspective and work of those actively engaged in these events. Teachers could join the networks based on interest and the demonstration of professional competence. Indeed the network could be an instrument for developing and certifying such competence.

Education networks of this kind would also not be able to function on their own to fulfill such a mission any more than a teacher as an individual can do so. Participants would need the time and resources to interact with political, cultural and economic entities. Education networks would also need to be supported by an administrative function. But, as in the case of Waldorf schools, the administration would be at the service of the basic educational functions rather than directing those functions.

Education networks as communities would differ from many existing professional organizations in two respects: 1) membership would be based on established competence, and 2) operated on a system of quality control. The course in Educational Assessment and Evaluation, described earlier as EA&E, presents a model of how such a network could function. The operation of each offering of EA&E is structured around a community of peers, developing their own and each other's' competencies as they carry out and produce research, instruction, curriculum, and assessments in ongoing conversation on general, as well as local, educational issues and problems. EA&E produces reports on attainment of competence by participants and is structured to produce educational products of general value. Quality control is maintained through the peer review process using the IQEA criteria (see Appendix B). EA&E deals only with fundamental educational competencies in educational assessment and evaluation, but similar programs could be designed on this model for any other or more advanced sets of competencies.

We have advocated the building of educational community around the activities of educational evaluation. This can occur *across* as well as *within* educational institutions. Programs such as EA&E demonstrate how participants, working from diverse educational institutions, can build professional capabilities and community, and carry out the activities of curriculum development, assessment and instruction across institutional boundaries. Moreover, EA&E presents a model for how teacher-based educational research can be conducted and what its goals should be. Without requiring centralization of authority, goal- and outcome-based reform aligned to core capabilities can foster autonomy within educational programs, build productive relationships across programs and institutions, while allowing freedom for teachers to practice teaching in accord with their insight, imagination, and professional experience. The basic functions of education can be provided by means other than via centralized authority and propagated other than via bureaucracies. Education networks can be organized around the free association of educators and educational stakeholders in the interests of learners, not subject primarily to the needs and rules of institutions. Practicing educators (i.e., those who are working directly with learners and learning goals, and so able to try out their ideas in practice) can and should be in a position of leadership in research-practitioner partnerships. Visit the *Forum for Educational Arts and Sciences* and follow the Forum Fellows' Initiative on Education Networks: http://EducationalRenewal.org/forum/fellows/

At present, most educational programs (except possibly those associated with well-endowed postsecondary education) do not, on their own, have the resources to carry out research into the fundamental questions that concern education. Public funding of research in education is critical. Private funding is, of course, invaluable, but if it is to be provided to public institutions, then it too must be conducted transparently and held publicly accountable for its ends and means. Instruments such as the National Assessment of Educational Progress (NAEP) and The Trends in International Mathematics and Science Study (TIMSS) can be used to assess vital signs in educational programs. Learning outcomes in publicly funded educational programs can be strategically sampled to create reports of the kind illustrated in the *Student to the State* sequence in Chapter III. Government is the natural choice to fund the R&D and professional development work of the education networks described above. The state can provide resources directed to assure that all individuals have equal access to educational opportunity. One of the reasons for the recently highlighted success of the Finnish educational system was that nation's commitment that all students would have access to the finest educational opportunities (Sahlberg, 2011). Read an expanded discussion of constructive role for government in education in the 2008 article by Paul Zachos and Robert M. Pruzek: http://acase.org/files/fedgovrole.pdf

Building Mathematical Foundations for Educational Information

Educational activities can be defined operationally as efforts to realize valued learning outcomes. The central information challenge in support of such efforts is producing actionable data in real-time instructional settings (i.e., information on how well targeted learning outcomes have been attained). The conceptual foundation for producing this information is the *practical learning goal* — that is, the statement of intended learning outcomes at a level of specificity appropriate for instruction. The most central educational research questions — e.g., the search for effects of methods of instruction — must rely on such information as the basis for their inferences.

Of particular value is information on how well core capabilities have been attained, as these hold the possibility of heightening and multiplying effects of learning. If we do not limit ourselves to outcome information on *knowledge* and *skills* but also consider information on *dispositions*, then we can begin to build the increasingly complete picture of the learner that is needed for emerging educational purposes.

Consider the case of *proportional reasoning,* a skill that may be considered a core capability in that it is prerequisite to competent participation in math, science, and technology in schoolwork, and to adequately grasping many contemporary economic and social issues.

> *The concept of proportionality is essential to understanding much in science, mathematics and technology. Many familiar variables such as speed, density and map scales are ratios or (rates) themselves.*

(American Association for the Advancement of Science (AAAS), 2001, p. 118)

Consider one aspect of proportional reasoning in particular — the ability to effectively coordinate two ratios to solve a problem. In the following case drawn from the **Cubes and Liquids**[35] assessment activity, proportional reasoning plays a role in predicting whether a solid object will float in a liquid. A successful prediction involves the coordination of the density of the solid object and the density of the liquid into which it is to be immersed. Densities of the objects and the liquids are each conceptualized as the ratios of their respective masses and volumes. The nature of the problem then is such that these two ratios need to be coordinated. **Figure 7.1** displays the results of an assessment based on this assessment activity.

---

[35] *http://acase.org/educational-assessment/*

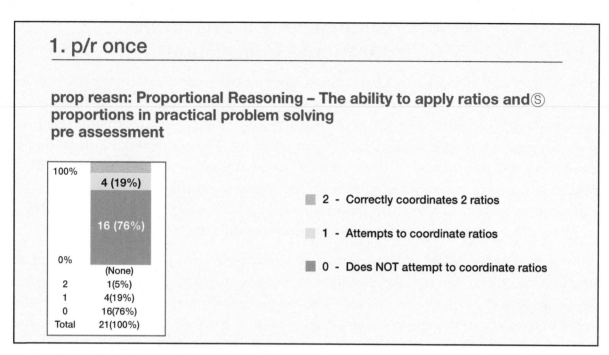

Figure 7.1 Basic information on attainment of a *practical learning outcome* at the level of a class

The high percentage of students who show no evidence of attainment of this capability indicates a need for instruction. In planning instruction for this group, the teacher will be interested in knowing how well individual students have attained the capability and how well the class as a whole performed on the task. This information is displayed in **Figure 7.2**.

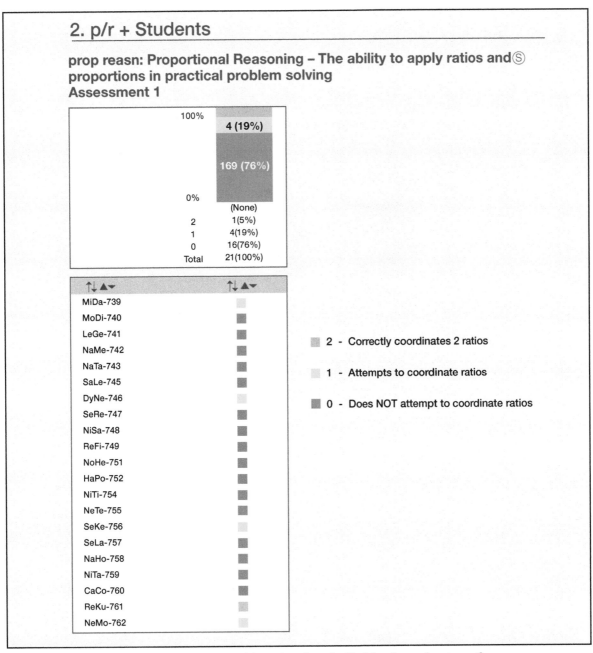

2. p/r + Students

prop reasn: Proportional Reasoning – The ability to apply ratios andⓈ
proportions in practical problem solving
Assessment 1

(None)	
2	1(5%)
1	4(19%)
0	16(76%)
Total	21(100%)

100% → 4 (19%)
169 (76%)
0%

↑↓▲▾	↑↓▲▾
MiDa-739	
MoDi-740	
LeGe-741	
NaMe-742	
NaTa-743	
SaLe-745	
DyNe-746	
SeRe-747	
NiSa-748	
ReFi-749	
NoHe-751	
HaPo-752	
NiTi-754	
NeTe-755	
SeKe-756	
SeLa-757	
NaHo-758	
NiTa-759	
CaCo-760	
ReKu-761	
NeMo-762	

2 - Correctly coordinates 2 ratios

1 - Attempts to coordinate ratios

0 - Does NOT attempt to coordinate ratios

Figure 7.2 Information enhanced by viewing individual student performance on a *practical learning outcome*

Having any information at all on student attainment of targeted learning goals can provide invaluable input for planning the next steps in instruction. As our long-time colleague and fellow ACASE founder, Tom Hick, has been known to say: "The data you have is the best data you have." But this leads inevitably and rightly to the question: How can this data be improved? One improvement would be to obtain an indication of how confident we can be in the assessment results. Multiple assessments of attainment of a learning goal can serve that purpose. As instruction progresses and additional assessments are conducted, the picture fills out, as in **Figure 7.3**.

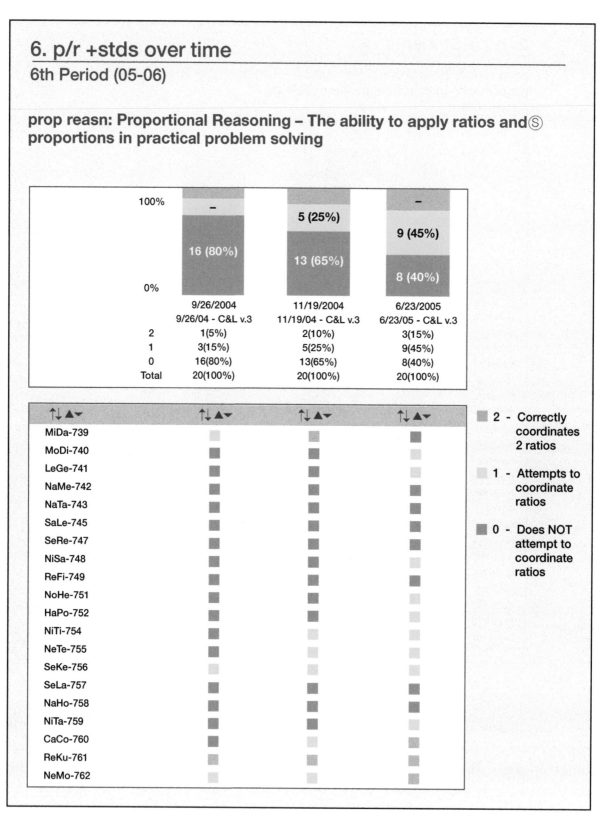

Figure 7.3 Further enhancement of educational information — performance on a *practical learning outcome* over time

The strength of our confidence in the individual ratings builds from additional assessment information as instruction proceeds. For those students who are rated at the same level of attainment on three occasions, we can be pleased with the reliability of our ratings, though not necessarily with the resulting attainment. A progression of ratings in the direction of red to yellow to green over time is also consistent with desired properties of the assessment instrument and so overall evidence begins to accumulate concerning reliability and validity of the assessment instrument. These all provide increasingly stronger indications for what is needed next in instruction.

The rating for the first student, MiDa, appears problematic. Did MiDa have a "bad day" in June? Did the teacher make an error in scoring the assessment results? Is there a flaw in the assessment instrument or process? Has instruction been inappropriate for this student in some way? Such a result calls for evaluation of one or more features of the educational activities underway.

As long as competence in proportional reasoning remains a targeted learning goal, such reports can continue to follow students through their careers, providing the critical information needed to plan, evaluate, and improve instruction. Imagine next year's science or mathematics teacher having this assessment information available as a basis for planning instruction for these same students. But can this information be improved further? Three questions can lead the way to consideration of how to improve educational information:

1. What level of attainment should be inferred for a student when results of multiple assessments are available? (For example, should the most recent level of attainment be preferred or is there another basis for making this inference?)

2. How can confidence in the judgment of attainment of a learning goal be enhanced?

3. How does the level of attainment on a given learning goal relate to the attainment of other learning goals and to the larger picture of the student's participation in the instructional environment?

To approach these, we would like to bring to the attention of all of our readers (not just educational specialists) a family of probabilistic analysis techniques known as *Bayesian statistics* (McGrayne, 2011; Phillips, 1973). These methods are geared to persistently refresh estimates of likelihood based on incoming data from many possible sources. A Bayesian analysis is able take the results of the three assessments of proportional reasoning shown and, based on some heuristic rule that we have devised, to assign a current level of probability of attainment to each of the three levels for every student.

For example, imagine characterizing some aspect of proportional reasoning as having three levels of attainment:

Level 2 — Attained

Level 1 — Progressing

Level 0 — No evidence of attainment

At which level is the student most likely functioning? The history of a student's attainment of these levels helps to draw a conclusion concerning the current level of attainment. But additional inputs drawn from a wider bank of information may also be helpful.

For example, the teacher may be privy to additional information concerning students' capabilities beyond this particular set of assessments. The teacher is likely to have additional information that supports or contradicts the results of an assessment and would wish that additional information to be taken into consideration. Bayesian methods welcome human judgment as supplement to other sources of data and can give weight to such judgments in a way that will best incorporate them into the overall picture of student attainment.

More specifically, a combined pool of information can be drawn on to estimate the probabilities that a student is functioning at each of these three levels. Probabilities are typically construed as ranging from 0.0 (representing certainty of non-occurrence) to 1.0 (representing certainty of occurrence). For our student A, the estimate of the probability of "attained" may be 0.23; the probability of being at the level "progressing" 0.74; and the probability "no evidence of attainment" is the best judgment is 0.03. The only constraint on these values is that the probabilities must add up to 1.0, i.e., be mutually exclusive and exhaustive for each student on a single learning goal. Each time additional information arrives concerning this learning goal, the analysis and its estimates of probability can be refreshed.

There are actually many additional sources of information that can be helpful in making a judgment as to level of attainment of a capability. The educational program may lodge more data on students' competence related to ratios (i.e., performing mathematical operations on fractions, percentages, etc.). Or it may be that students who studied with a particular seventh-grade mathematics teacher tend to be particularly strong in working with ratios and proportions. Here is a place where the enormous banks of information concerning students that are lodged in schools may become of practical value — attendance, interests, dispositions, grades given by different teachers, performance on various tests and survey instruments, all could be incorporated via a Bayesian analysis to enrich the estimate of probability that a student is performing at some level of attainment of a capability. By incorporating such information from performance on other learning goals and other relevant features of the instructional environment, stronger and stronger estimates can be obtained to help the teacher know how likely it is that a student is performing at a particular level of attainment. This is with essentially no additional effort on the part of the teacher beyond calling up the most recent assessment results for any given learning goal. Sound human insight and judgment, which should always be at the heart of decision-making, can now enjoy a lively interaction with complex sources of information through data analytic processes devoted to estimating with increasing precision how well targeted learning goals have been attained by individuals and groups.

Figure 7.4 shows how this information would be displayed to help a teacher plan the next step of instruction related to proportional reasoning for student W,R and the class as a whole.

The left hand portion of **Figure 7.4** displays assessment results on attainment of proportional reasoning for a class and for student W,R on three different occasions. On the basis of these three assessments alone, one might judge that the student has attained the top level of performance on this learning goal. However, the *Current Probability* levels on the right hand side of the graph, calculated from a computerized algorithm that incorporates additional sources of information, suggests that this may not be the case. Moreover, the Your Assessment buttons, which are the teacher's means for incorporating an independent judgment into the analysis, shows that the teacher is about to enter and save a rating that differs from the rating based on the July 23 assessment results. Apparently, she is privy to information that contradicts the most recent assessment results. When she enters and saves her rating, the *Current Probability* will likely strengthen the algorithm-based results. But actually there may be no need for her to intervene with a rating expressing her personal judgment, as the arrow in **Figure 7.4** shows she is about to do. The computational algorithm that generates probabilities for the levels of attainment already has come to the same conclusion that she has — that the likelihood is quite low that the student is actually functioning at the level indicated by the July assessment results. But why should the student have been given an incorrect rating? Was it a slip of a rater's finger? A fault in the assessment rubric? Is the same happening with other students as well? The teacher has indications here that suggest the need to reconsider the validity and reliability of the measures used. But there is another possibility. What if there is persistent disagreement between the teacher and the probability algorithm concerning the best estimate of student level of attainment? Perhaps the algorithm itself needs to be revised or refreshed.

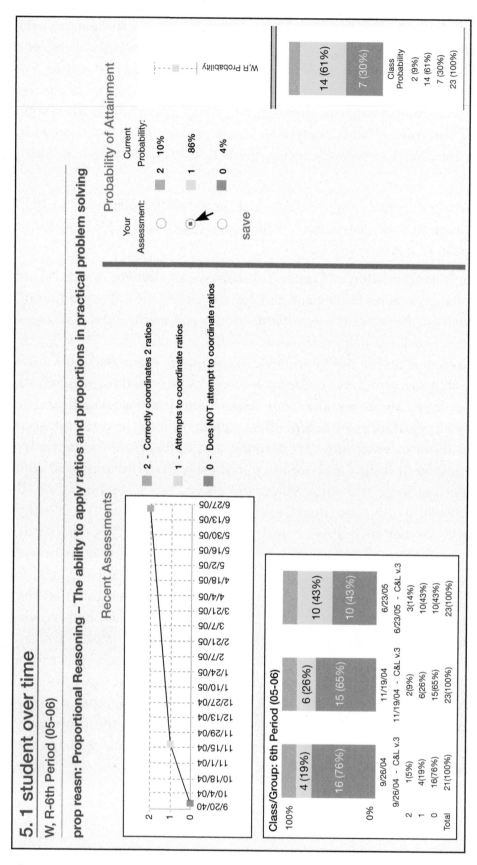

Figure 7.4 Assessment results enhanced with estimates of probability of attainment

This may seem an inordinate amount of attention given to a single capability, but it actually is precisely the necessary step forward. We must identify core capabilities, set aligned learning goals, build valid ways to assess their attainment, and have an indication of our confidence in assessment results to compose a useful picture of the degree to which learners have attained intended learning outcomes. Furthermore, we must study the relationships between these capabilities. How do they inter-depend? What effect might the attainment of one learning outcome have on the attainment of others? This is precisely the type of information that is currently missing in attempts to answer simple questions such as — which methods of instruction and which program characteristics are most effective in facilitating attainment? The *Student to the State* sequence presented earlier shows how this very information can support policy planning and decision-making up and down educational institution hierarchies. Perhaps more importantly, each such piece of information increases our depth of knowing and understanding the learner.

Information on the relationship between practical learning outcomes is the needed direction to be taken for enriching educational research, as well as for supporting decision-making and action at the scene of educational events. Such relationships, possibly hierarchical and causal, could be a foundation for establishing an empirical basis for what we have been calling *learning progressions* (Heritage, 2008; Schneider & Plasman, 2011) and also could serve as the basis for operationalizing Mauritz Johnson's notion of a *goal contribution unit* (Johnson, 1985).

Information technology now permits not only the analysis of immense quantities of information of this kind, but also extensive data entry options. A teacher can enter assessment ratings onto a mobile application while instruction is underway. Students can perform tasks and respond to questions on computers, clickers, and other mobile devices. The teacher (and students) can obtain near-real-time estimates of student attainment of targeted learning goals. Consider the full history of information that is regularly collected and stored regarding any particular student in existing school systems. Once coordinated with results concerning practical learning goals and outcomes, vast pools of information can be made productive at many levels of decision-making. Bayesian methods can turn big data into data that is just the right size for practical decision-making. Those interested in collaborating in this project will find resources and colleagues at the Forum for Educational Arts and Sciences. http://EducationalRenewal.org/forum/fellows/

In the larger picture, such mathematical models and data analytics must always be the servants of purely educational purposes; institutional needs must not take priority over purely educational considerations. Nor, as John Tukey warns (Tukey, 1969), do we wish to bow to theories and methods that were developed for other purposes, particularly, in the case of the field of education, the norm-referenced testing paradigm that was developed for non-educational psychometric purposes. Moreover, please consider again the caveat that has accompanied all of our presentations in *Knowing the Learner:* Information on how well learning goals have been attained should not be used for non-educational purposes. When this point of view is adopted, it also becomes clear that it is not the internal features of tests — e.g., test items and right and wrong answers — that need to be kept secure, but rather information concerning individual students, so that it will not be misused. Generally speaking, we can conclude that information on student attainment is likely to be misused if it is being put to non-educational purposes. In attempting to understand the nature and actions of others, it is critical to never lapse into making another human being, teacher or student, simply an object of observation. We must exercise the same reverence for the other, the same respect for freedom and personal privilege that we would wish extended to ourselves.

Concluding Thoughts

Educational assessment is essentially an act of knowing the learner; it is also a learning activity for the teacher. *Educational evaluation* is the act of using information to best help learners attain worthy learning outcomes.

Curriculum, assessment, instruction, and evaluation are expressions of our personal and cultural values. Comprehensive evaluation then (i.e., the thorough ongoing review of curriculum, assessment, instruction, and evaluation) gives us a way to become more aware of ourselves and our culture, as well as to better know our students.

We have argued that assessment of attainment of distinct learning goals at the critical level of specificity provides the primary information need for evaluation and improvement of educational practice.

The worthiness of intended learning outcomes is the primary concern of curriculum development. We have offered several suggestions concerning *curriculum development:*

1. The need to extend the borders of curriculum so that they encompass the full human being through attention to skills and dispositions as well as to knowledge

2. The need for the sake of efficiency to focus on *core capabilities*

3. The need to be sensitive to the developmental levels of learners and to their current levels of attainment on core capabilities

4. Creative engagement in curriculum development, i.e., setting learning goals, which can be both an inspiring and revitalizing activity for teachers

We have had little to say regarding the desirability of particular *instructional* practices because we believe that such decisions are best left to competent and qualified teachers, and because we know that the choice of appropriate instruction depends very much on the unique constellation of learning goals, learners, and the cultural contexts in which teachers and learners find themselves.

We have emphasized and affirmed the sovereignty of the meeting of teacher and student as a place of creative action. We have said little concerning learning processes themselves, although irrefutably the enrichment of such processes may be considered the heart of the educational enterprise. Rather, we have attempted to open pathways of productive information leading to and away from educational events, supporting educational activities and the individuals who guide them. It will be on the basis of assessment results aligned to practical learning goals that the field of education will be able to establish concrete facts about learning such as the ones that Roediger, McDaniel, and their colleagues have accumulated (Brown et al., 2014), or as many are currently attempting to do regarding physiological and neurological correlates to learning.

We have identified what we believe are critical professional competencies that are needed to grasp and take thoughtful action on educational questions at all levels. We have provided methods for developing these capabilities. We have noted the need to validate the choice and usefulness of these competencies through research based on their relevance to facilitating the attainment of practical learning outcomes aligned with core capabilities. In this way, professional development is no different from any other educational activity.

Reaping the full and most humane benefits of educational information requires that assessment be purely devoted to knowing the learner, that evaluation be undertaken in an atmosphere of mutual trust focused on helping learners to realize their potentials through the improvement of educational programs and activities.

The more we can experience the concepts, skills, and dispositions of the other with a view towards appreciation and support, the greater will be our success and our reward in the outcome. Rather than focusing merely on giving students rewards for learning, we can reward ourselves immeasurably by learning to know the learner.

Appendix A
12 Fundamental Learning Goals for Educational Assessment and Evaluation

1. Uses the concept of the learning goal to identify the end towards which all educational processes/activities are directed

2. Uses the concept of the learning goal to distinguish assessment from the other essential features of educational processes/activities

3. Uses the concept of the learning goal to distinguish instruction from the other essential features of educational processes/activities

4. Applies the concept of the critical level of specificity to educational planning and decision-making, i.e., distinguishes broader learning goals from those specified at a level appropriate for lessons and units of instruction

5. Applies the concept of core capabilities to educational planning and decision-making

6. Applies the distinction between domains of learning to educational planning and decision-making

7. Distinguishes educational assessment from testing and grading

8. Distinguishes educational assessment from educational evaluation

9. Brings concern for the notion of validity to challenges and problems in assessment and evaluation

10. Brings concern for the notion of reliability to challenges and problems in assessment and evaluation

11. Applies assessment information to evaluate educational activities

12. Applies assessment information to build community

Levels of Attainment

For the 12 Fundamental EA&E Learning Goals

3. Spontaneously applies the concept (extends the stipulated definition to new situations)

2. Competently applies the concept (competently applies the stipulated definition in directed activities)

1. Applies the concept (but does not give evidence of competence in applying the stipulated definition)

0. No evidence of attainment of the concept

Appendix B
Indicators of Quality for Educational Activities (IQEA)

Overview: What is the IQEA?

The IQEA is one of the two primary instructional resources for the workshops in Educational Assessment and Evaluation (EA&E)[1]. The other is the set of 12 Learning Fundamental Educational Assessment and Evaluation Learning Goals that are presented in Appendix A. Workshop participants develop, carry out, and evaluate *Educational Projects* composed of the four fundamental educational activities — curriculum, assessment, instruction, and evaluation, using the IQEA as a guideline. Their progress is documented in a series of *Evaluation Reports*. Participants support each other's work through periodic review of each other's Educational Projects. Through this process, participants become competent practitioners in educational assessment and evaluation.

The IQEA criteria presented in the rating scales below are used by course participants and instructors, in a process of peer review, to evaluate the Educational Projects. For instructional purposes, a separate Evaluation Report is prepared for every distinct learning goal. The evaluation criteria are implemented on the ACASE online Assessment Information System[2] in a form that facilitates rating, review of reliability of assessments, and reports of student attainment.

The purpose of the IQEA is to foster practices that build competence in assessment and evaluation and increase the quality and value of curriculum, assessment, instruction, and evaluation.

How to Use the IQEA

Evaluation Reports

Evaluation Reports contain the following:

- The name/title of the Educational Activity

- Names and affiliation/s of Developer/s

- The Learning Goal around which the report is centered. Specify whether the Learning Goal is a Concept (C), Skill (S), or a Disposition (D)

---

[1] *http://educationalrenewal.org/forum/courses/*

[2] *http://www.scientificinquiry.org/login.asp*

Each Evaluation Report centers on one learning goal and must include all of the following:

1. Curriculum

    a. A learning goal specified at a level appropriate for assessment and instruction (practical learning goal)

    b. A justification of the learning goal by reference to standards or other bases for evaluation (e.g., research, reasoning based on evidence or past experience)

    c. An explanation of appropriateness of the learning goal for the students to be served

2. Assessment Methods—Directions for replicable administration of the assessment instrument/activities aligned to the learning goal

3. Instruction:

    a. A description of the instructional methods aligned to the learning goal

    b. An explanation of appropriateness of the instruction for the students to be served

4. Reports on how well the learning goal has been attained by individual students and relevant groups

5. An evaluation of each of the above features after each assessment of the attainment of the learning goal

The three Evaluation Reports provide evidence of participant attainment of the 12 Fundamental Learning Goals by EA&E participants in three different domains of learning.

Grading Scheme

The contents of Evaluation Reports and peer review discussions based on IQEA ratings serve as the basis for assigning grades to participants in EA&E courses and workshops.

Instructors and assigned peers will evaluate the learning activities presented in the Evaluation Reports on several occasions specified by the instructor. A date is set for final peer reviews of the Evaluation Reports, after which each course participant prepares a final Evaluation Report for each Learning Goal and submits the reports to the instructor. These final Evaluation Reports become the basis upon which the instructor assigns final grades.

Bold items represent the level of accomplishment expected for the final ER.

Italic items represent the level of accomplishment required for intermediate-level reports.

Final Grade

A   Bold level reached on all criteria for all three Evaluation Reports

B   Bold level reached on all criteria for two Evaluation Reports. Italic level reached on the third (this is the level that must be reached in occasions where a stipend is offered for participation.)

C   Bold level reached on all criteria for one Evaluation Report, italic on the others

D   Italic level reached on all criteria for all three learning goals

F   Italic level not reached on all criteria

Intermediate Grades

A   Italic level reached on all criteria of all three Evaluation Reports

B   Italic level reached on all criteria of two Evaluation Reports. (Level of accomplishment needed to receive any stipends associated with participation)

C   Italic level reached on all criteria for one Evaluation Report

D   Italic level not reached on all criteria for any Evaluation Report

Scales for Rating the Indicators of Quality

Ratings/judgments must be based on evidence of accomplishment. If no evidence is available, the indicator must be rated at the lowest level.

Part 1: Planning

Curriculum (Learning Goals)

A) Practical

1. ***The learning goal has been specified at the level of a practical learning goal***

0. The learning goal has not been specified at the level of specificity of a learning goal

Rubric (We use the term rubric to refer to descriptions or explanations of what evidence is needed to assign a specified rating level): practical learning goals (aka learning objectives) are written at a level appropriate for and specific to individual lessons or units, as opposed to broad learning goals. The presence of a perfectly aligned assessment can be a good indicator of the desired level of specificity.

B) Justified

    2. The learning goal is effectively justified

    1. *The learning goal is justified*

    0. The learning goal is not justified

Rubric: learning goals are justified or substantiated by being explicitly referenced to state/national standards and/or appropriate research. Reference to expert judgments and insights is also a basis for justification. The personal research of a teacher can also be a basis justification or substantiation.

C) Core Capabilities—Critical Foundation for Learning

    3. Clearly a core learning capability (substantiated by research)

    2. Likely a core learning capability (substantiated by recognized authority)

    1. *Possibly a core learning capability (sound argument provided)*

    0. No evidence that the learning goal refers to a core learning capability

Rubric: Core capabilities are those that support concurrent and subsequent learning or that generalize to contribute to effectiveness in the world, e.g., real-world problem solving.

Assessment Plan

D) Validity

    4. The learning goal is aligned with four or more appropriate assessments

    3. The learning goal is aligned with three appropriate assessments

    2. *The learning goal is aligned with two appropriate assessments*

    1. The learning goal is aligned with one appropriate assessment

    0. The learning goal is not aligned with appropriate assessments

Rubric: A valid assessment is one that provides precisely the information that is needed to judge whether the learning goal has been attained. The term "appropriate" is used here to represent the rater's perception of validity. This is often referred to as "apparent validity" or "face validity."

E) Replicability

    3. Three assessment activities are each presented in a way that is conducive to easy and reliable replication

    2. *Two assessment activities are each presented in a way that is conducive to easy and reliable replication*

1. One assessment activity is presented in a way that is conducive to easy and reliable replication

0. The assessment activities are written and/or formatted in a way that is not conducive to easy and reliable replication or no assessment activities are presented.

Instructional Plan

F) Instruction Relevant to Learning Goal

2. **The instructional plan is clearly directed to supporting students' attainment of the learning goal**

1. *The instructional plan appears to be directed to supporting students' attainment of the learning goal*

0. The instructional plan does not appear clearly directed to supporting students' attainment of the learning goal

Part 2: Implementation

The Assessment Process

G) Results are presented by practical learning outcomes

1. ***Assessment results are presented at the level of practical learning outcomes***

0. Assessment results are not presented at the level of practical learning outcomes

H) Assessment Results Are Presented by Individual Student

4. Results of four or more of the assessment results are presented by individual student

3. **Three of the assessment results are presented by individual student**

2. *Two of the assessment results are presented by individual student*

1. One of the assessment results is presented by individual student

0. None of the assessment results are presented by individual student

Rubric: Assessment results should be presented by individual student. The presentation may be graphic, numerical, narrative, or some combination. [The ACASE online Assessment Information System (AIS) provides the capacity to easily generate graphic and numerical reports for individual students as well as groups of interest.]

I) Multiple Assessment Opportunities

    4. The learning goal was assessed on four or more occasions

    3. **The learning goal was assessed on three occasions**

    2. *The learning goal was assessed on two occasions*

    1. The learning goal was assessed on one occasion

    0. The learning goal was not assessed

Rubric: This can include assessments conducted before, during, and after instruction.

Part 3: Evaluation

J) Integration of Assessment Activity with Instruction

    4. Four or more of the assessment activities take place in the living context of instruction, i.e., without taking time away from instruction

    3. Three of the assessment activities take place in the living context of instruction, i.e., without taking time away from instruction

    2. **Two of the assessment activities take place in the living context of instruction, i.e., without taking time away from instruction**

    1. *One of the assessment activities takes place in the living context of instruction, i.e., without taking time away from instruction*

    0. None of the assessment activities take place in the living context of instruction, i.e., without taking time away from instruction

K) Timeliness of Assessment Results

    4. Assessment results were available in time to plan the next steps of instruction in four or more cases

    3. Assessment results were available in time to plan the next steps of instruction in three cases

    2. **Assessment results were available in time to plan the next steps of instruction in two cases**

    1. *Assessment results were available in time to plan the next steps of instruction in one case*

    0. Assessment results were not available in time to plan the next steps of instruction in any cases

L) Assessment Activities Produce Actionable Information Based on Levels
of Student Attainment

    4. Assessments activities have produced actionable information based on levels of student attainment in four or more cases

    3. Assessments activities have produced actionable information based on levels of student attainment in three cases

    2. **Assessments activities have produced actionable information based on levels of student attainment in two cases**

    1. *Assessments activities have produced actionable information based on levels of student attainment in one case*

    0. Assessment activities have not produced actionable information based on levels of student attainment

Rubric: Actionable information is information that can be used to improve educational activities and programs. The strongest evidence of actionability is the demonstration that assessment results were found useful in deliberations concerning program evaluation and improvement.

M) Reliability

    4. Reliability studies have been conducted and reported for four or more assessment activities

    3. Reliability studies have been conducted for three assessment activities

    2. **Reliability studies have been conducted for two assessment activities**

    1. *Reliability studies have been conducted for one assessment activity*

    0. Reliability studies have not been conducted for any assessment activities

Rubric: Evidence that demonstrates how the reliability of assessment results was determined must be presented. A simple, straightforward way to do this is to have multiple raters or judges conduct assessments of a reasonably sized sample of student performances at different levels of student attainment. The AIS provides a reliability feature for comparing the judgments of multiple raters.

N) Using Assessment and Evaluation Reports to Build Community

    3. **Evaluation reports, including assessment results, have been presented at meetings including faculty, administration, and the larger school community**

    2. *Evaluation reports, including assessment results, have been presented at meetings at which faculty and administration were present*

1. Evaluation reports, including assessment results, have been presented to colleagues

0. Evaluation reports have not been presented at meetings

O) State of Learning Goals

1. ***Assessment results have been applied to produce inferences, conclusions, and recommendations that improve the educational activity's learning goals***

0. There is no evidence that assessment results have been applied to produce inferences, conclusions, and recommendations to improve the educational activity's learning goals

P) State of Assessment Instruments

1. ***Assessment results have been applied to produce inferences, conclusions, and recommendations to improve assessment activities***

0. There is no evidence that assessment results have been applied to produce inferences, conclusions, and recommendations to improve assessment activities

Q) State of Instructional Methods

1. ***Assessment results have been applied to produce inferences, conclusions, and recommendations to improve methods of instruction***

0. There is no evidence that assessment results have been applied to produce inferences, conclusions, and recommendations to improve methods of instruction

R) Evaluation of Student Engagement in Instruction

5. Student engagement in instruction was evaluated on at least four occasions

4. Student engagement in instruction was evaluated on three occasions

3. **Student engagement in instruction was evaluated on two occasions**

2. Student engagement in instruction was evaluated on one occasion

1. *Methods for evaluating student engagement in instruction <u>have</u> been developed*

0. Methods for evaluating student engagement in instruction <u>have not</u> been developed

S) Evaluation of Student Engagement in the Assessment Activities

  5. Student engagement in assessment was evaluated on at least four occasions

  4. Student engagement in assessment was evaluated on three occasions

  3. **Student engagement in assessment was evaluated on two occasions**

  2. Student engagement in assessment was evaluated on one occasion

  1. *Methods for evaluating student engagement in assessment <u>have</u> been developed*

  0. Methods for evaluating student engagement in assessment <u>have not</u> been developed

Appendix C
Learning Objectives AGEO 110

The Search for Life Beyond the Earth
Professor John Delano

Learning Objectives AGEO 110

What is Life? Aqueous chemical system

1. Refers to aqueous chemical system

0. No evidence of attainment

Not Rated

What is Life? Capable of evolution

1. Refers to being capable of evolution

0. No evidence of attainment

Not Rated

What is Life? Information-rich molecules

1. Refers to information-rich molecules

0. No evidence of attainment

Not Rated

What is Life? Carbon-based system

1. Refers to carbon-based system

0. No evidence of attainment

Not Rated

What is Life? Reproduction

1. Refers to reproduction

0. No evidence of attainment

Not Rated

What is Life? Low entropy system

1. Refers to low entropy system

0. No evidence of attainment

Not Rated

Conditions for Life-Restricted Temperature range

1. Refers to Restricted Temperature range

0. No evidence of attainment

Not Rated

Conditions for Life-Restricted Pressure range

1. Refers to Restricted Pressure range

0. No evidence of attainment

Not Rated

Conditions for Life-Source(s) of nutrients	1. Refers to Source(s) of nutrients
	0. No evidence of attainment
	Not Rated
Conditions for Life-Geological times	1. Refers to Geological times
	0. No evidence of attainment
	Not Rated
Conditions for Life-Planet/Satellite system	1. Refers to Planet/Satellite system
	0. No evidence of attainment
	Not Rated
Conditions for Life-Liquid water	1. Refers to Liquid water
	0. No evidence of attainment
	Not Rated
Conditions for Life-Synthesis of molecules analogs for life's function (e.g., DNA and RNA analogs)	1. Refers to Synthesis of molecules for life's function
	0. No evidence of attainment
	Not Rated
Conditions for Life-Absence of (or protection against) planet-sterilizing events	1. Refers to Absence of (or protection against) planet-sterilizing events
	0. No evidence of attainment
	Not Rated
Conditions for Life-Object of 0.5-5.0 Earth mass	1. Refers to Object of 0.5-5.0 Earth mass
	0. No evidence of attainment
	Not Rated
Conditions for Life-Habitable/Goldilocks zone	1. Refers to Habitable/Goldilocks zone
	0. No evidence of attainment
	Not Rated
Conditions for Life-Long-lived, stable star	1. Refers to Long-lived, stable star
	0. No evidence of attainment
	Not Rated
Conditions for Life-Terrestrial vs. Extra T	1. Refers to Terrestrial vs. Extra T
	0. No evidence of attainment
	Not Rated
Drake Equation-Infers Correct Units	4. Infers correct units in 4 cases
	3. Infers correct units in 3 cases

2. Infers correct units in 2 cases

1. Infers correct units in 1 case

0. Infers correct units in 0 cases

Not Rated

Knowledgeable estimates of astronomical scale

8. Gives 8 knowledgeable estimates

7. Gives 7 knowledgeable estimates

6. Gives 6 knowledgeable estimates

5. Gives 5 knowledgeable estimates

4. Gives 4 knowledgeable estimates

3. Gives 3 knowledgeable estimates

2. Gives 2 knowledgeable estimates

1. Gives 1 knowledgeable estimates

0. Gives 0 knowledgeable estimates

Not Rated

Chooses whole numbers when appropriate

2. Chooses whole numbers when appropriate in 2 cases

1. Chooses whole numbers when appropriate in 1 case

0. Chooses whole numbers when appropriate in 0 cases

Not Rated

Chooses fractions when appropriate

2. Chooses fractions when appropriate in 2 cases

1. Chooses fractions when appropriate in 1 case

0. Chooses fractions when appropriate in 0 cases

Not Rated

Correctly selects inverse relationship

2. Correctly selects inverse relationship in 2 cases

1. Correctly selects inverse relationship in 1 case

0. Correctly selects inverse relationship in 0 cases

Not Rated

Correctly selects direct relationship

1. Correctly selects direct relationship in 1 case

0. Correctly selects direct relationship in 0 cases

Not Rated

Consistency of graph choice and justification

3. Graph and justification are consistent in 3 cases

2. Graph and justification are consistent in 2 cases

1. Graph and justification are consistent in 1 case

0. Graph and justification are consistent in 0 cases

Not Rated

Appendix D
Assessment Instrument AGEO 110

Signature: _____

Printed name: _____

The Search for Life Beyond the Earth

(Fall 2010; MWF at 9:20-10:15 AM; LC 1)

Professor John Delano Version 1

Instructions: These questions are intended to give me some idea about your current mathematical skills and scientific knowledge. I will use this information to evaluate how to direct my instruction most effectively. Although you are ***NOT*** being graded on these questions, please respond to the best of your ability so that the topics in this course can be designed to best suit the class's preparation. Please write legibly. Thank you.

1. What do you have to take into consideration to address the question *'What is life'*? Please explain your answer in the space provided below.

_____

_____

_____

_____

_____

2. What do you have to take into consideration to address the question *'What conditions are needed for life to form'*? Please explain your answer in the space provided below.

_____

_____

_____

_____

_____

3. What do you have to take into consideration to address the question *'How common is life beyond the Earth'*? Please explain your answer in the space provided below.

_____

_____

_____

_____

_____

(for Questions #4, 5): The Drake equation for estimating the number of technologically advanced, communicative civilizations in the galaxy is the following: $N = S * f_{planet} * n_e * f_{life} * f_{intell} * f_{tech} * L$ where S = number of stars in the galaxy, f_{planet} = fraction of stars with planets; n_e = for stars with planets, how many planets per star are potentially habitable; f_{life} = fraction of those potentially habitable planets that actually have life; f_{intell} = fraction of those life-bearing planets where complex, intelligent life formed; f_{tech} = fraction of those planets with intelligent life that actually develop the technology to communicate with radio waves; L = fraction of a star's lifespan when the communicating civilization exists.

4. If the first 4 terms (only $S * f_{planet} * n_e * f_{life}$) in the Drake equation were multiplied together, what would be the units (e.g., number of Earth-like planets/star; number of habitable planets/galaxy) on a resulting number? Please explain your answer briefly.

_____
_____
_____
_____
_____

5. What are your own best estimates for values of the following terms in the Drake equation?

Minimum likely value of **S**: _____ Maximum likely value of **S**: _____

Minimum likely value of f_{planet}: _____ Maximum likely value of f_{planet}: _____

Minimum likely value of n_e: _____ Maximum likely value of n_e: _____

Minimum likely value of f_{life}: _____ Maximum likely value of f_{life}: _____

(for Questions #6 — 8): The following equation is used to estimate the surface temperature, T in degrees Kelvin, on a planet orbiting a star at a distance, R in meters. L = luminosity of the star in watts; A = fraction of star's energy arriving at the planet that is reflected back into space; 16πs are constants.

$$T(R) = \left(\frac{L(1-A)}{16\pi\sigma R^2} \right)^{\frac{1}{4}} \text{ degrees Kelvin (K)}$$

6. ***If L and A were held constant***, which graph below would best represent the relationship between a planet's surface temperature, T, and its distance, R, from the star? Please circle your choice of graph, and briefly explain your reasoning.

(Circle one)　　***Graph A***　　　***Graph B***　　　***Graph C***

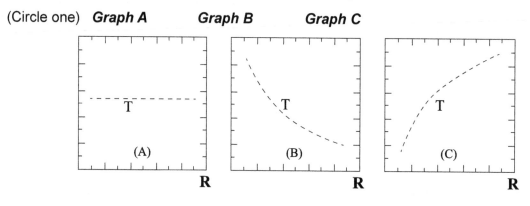

_____
_____
_____
_____
_____

$$T(R) = \left(\frac{L(1-A)}{16\pi\sigma R^2} \right)^{\frac{1}{4}} \text{ degrees Kelvin (K)}$$

7. ***If L and R were held constant***, which graph below would best represent the relationship between a planet's surface temperature, T, and the planet's reflectivity, A? Please circle your choice of graph, and briefly explain your reasoning.

(Circle one)　　***Graph A***　　　***Graph B***　　　***Graph C***

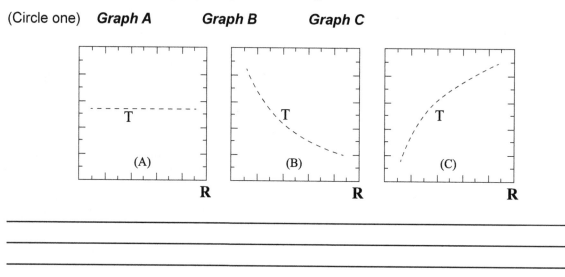

_____
_____
_____
_____
_____

$$T(R) = \left(\frac{L(1-A)}{16\pi\sigma R^2} \right)^{\frac{1}{4}} \text{ degrees Kelvin (K)}$$

8. If A and R were held constant, which graph below would best represent the relationship between a star's luminosity, L, and a planet's surface temperature, T? Please circle your choice of graph, and briefly explain your reasoning.

(Circle one)   *Graph A*   *Graph B*   *Graph C*

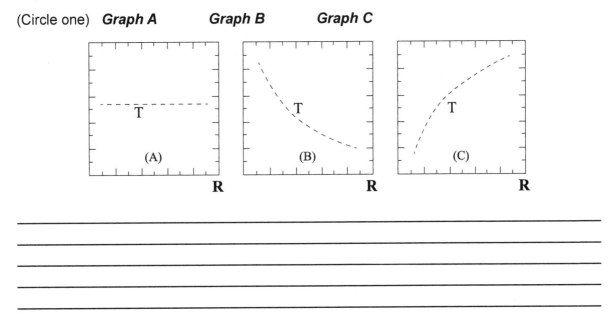

(A)   (B)   (C)

R   R   R

_____

_____

_____

_____

_____

Appendix E
Carol Ann Tomlinson's *Invitations to Learn*

From *Educational Leadership* | September 2002 | Volume 60 | Number 1

Affirmation

- I am accepted and acceptable here just as I am.

- I am safe here — physically, emotionally, and intellectually.

- People here care about me.

- People here listen to me.

- People know how I'm doing, and it matters to them that I do well.

- People acknowledge my interests and perspectives and act upon them.

Contribution

- I make a difference in this place.

- I bring unique and valuable perspectives and abilities to this place.

- I help other students and the entire class to succeed.

- I am connected to others through mutual work on common goals.

Purpose

- I understand what we do here.

- I see significance in what we do.

- What we do reflects me and my world.

- The work we do makes a difference in the world.

- The work absorbs me.

Power

- What I learn here is useful to me now.

- I make choices that contribute to my success.

- I know what quality looks like and how to create quality work here.

- Dependable support for my journey exists in this classroom.

Challenge

- The work here complements my ability.

- The work stretches me.

- I work hard in this classroom.

- When I work hard, I generally succeed.

- I am accountable for my own growth, and I contribute to the growth of others.

- I accomplish things here that I didn't believe were possible.

Glossary

Aggregation — This term is used in two very different senses:

1. *Aggregation across discrete learning outcomes* — for example, aggregating assessment items to obtain an overall test score. This is the traditional/conventional process of combining ratings or test items in order to return a single (aggregate) number (often a weighted sum) that is intended to reflect performance or quality. This type of aggregation provides a simpler or more compact view of overall performance, but sacrifices the information needed to inform instructional planning and educational improvement decisions in general.

2. *Aggregation of discrete learning outcomes across groups* — for example, aggregating assessment results such as the proportion of students who attained a learning outcome in a class, school, or state. As long as the discrete nature of the learning outcome (i.e., alignment to a discrete learning goal) is maintained, aggregation across groups maintains the information needed for evaluation, planning, and decision-making at its respective level of aggregation. Such information may be disaggregated to see how members of population subgroups (e.g., gender) are performing. This type of information and aggregation can be used to support instructional planning, evaluation, resource allocation, and professional development.

Assessment — see *Educational Assessment*

Core Capabilities — Capabilities that provide a foundation for concurrent learning, future learning, and productive application to situations that will be met outside of the educational setting. Core capabilities may have a moral, logical, or empirical basis. Moral in that they represent a valued human quality or attribute that can be developed through education, e.g., the ability to read. Logical in that there is reason to believe that the targeted capability will have the desired relationship to concurrent and future learning, and application outside of school settings. Empirical when this relationship has been demonstrated through research.

Critical Level of Specificity — The level of specificity at which a learning goal is useful for planning, carrying out, and evaluating instruction.

Curriculum — The set of learning goals underlying an educational activity or program. "A structured set of intended learning outcomes" (Johnson, 1977).

Disaggregation — *See Aggregation*

Educational Activities — taken in a comprehensive sense includes, or should include, the fundamental features of educational processes — curriculum, assessment,

150

instruction, and evaluation. Johnson has shown how such features each have *distinct planning, implementation,* and *evaluation* aspects (Johnson, 1977).

Educational Assessment — Obtaining, analyzing, and presenting information on how well discrete learning goals have been attained. The word assessment, as used in *Knowing the Learner*, generally has this meaning.

Educational Evaluation — The practice of applying information (assessment results and other information) in planning and decision-making to increase the value of educational activities and programs. The word *evaluation*, as used in *Knowing the Learner*, always has this meaning. More specifically, we can think of working to improve all of the inferences, conclusions, generalizations, value judgments, and decisions that arise from systematic examination of educational programs, activities, and outcomes.

Educational Events — The interactions in time and space between teacher and learner directed to realizing (helping learners attain) learning goals. They are meetings around the theme of one or more learning goals. *Educational events* are the special moments when efforts are being made to realize the attainment of learning goals. Why must educational events include learning goals? This is because explicitly or not, consciously or not, educational activities are directed primarily to the attainment of capabilities. Learning goals represent those desired capabilities.

Educational Settings — The physical locations in which the learner is found during educational events.

Educational Programs — The formal venues for providing educational activities — e.g., institutions such as primary schools and universities, formal courses of study, but also training programs, workshops, MOOCs, etc.

Evaluation — see *Educational Evaluation*

Empirical (adv. Empirically) — Based on or verifiable by observation or experience. This is as opposed to judgments based exclusively on authority, tradition, or logic. Piaget was fond of replying to conventional assertions concerning psychology or education by saying, "It's an empirical question," meaning that it is a matter to be investigated systematically and through direct experience.

High-Stakes, Norm-Referenced testing and grading (HSNR) — In general, **high stakes** means that test scores are used to determine punishments (such as sanctions, penalties, funding reductions, negative publicity), accolades (awards, public celebration, positive publicity), advancement (grade promotion or graduation for students), or compensation (salary increases or bonuses for administrators and teachers). From the *Glossary of Educational Reform:*
http://edglossary.org/high-stakes-testing/

Norm-referenced refers to standardized tests that are designed to compare and rank test takers in relation to one another. Norm-referenced tests report whether test takers performed better or worse than a hypothetical average student, which is determined by comparing scores against the performance results of a statistically selected group of test takers, typically of the same age or grade level, who have already taken the exam. From the *Glossary of Educational Reform:* http://edglossary.org/norm-referenced-test/

Note that we do not feel that this practice is limited to standardized tests, but is a central feature of conventional testing and grading in general.

Instruction — Any effort made, directly in relationship with learners, to help them attain one or more learning goals. In other words, anything that is done directly with a student to support the attainment of a learning goal.

Intended Learning Outcome — see *Learning Goal*

Learning Goal (also Intended Learning Outcome) — A statement of the intention to develop or facilitate the attainment of a human capability, e.g., a concept, skill, or disposition.

Practical Learning Goal — A discrete learning goal stated at a level of specificity appropriate for instruction.

Practical Learning Outcome — Assessment results associated or aligned with a practical learning goal.

Rubric — A descriptive or explanatory guide (often with examples) to the levels of attainment of a practical learning goal or outcome.

Tests (Conventional) — Instruments in which student performance on items reflecting diverse learning goals are given values (typically numeric) and then summed to yield a total score.

References

Abeles, Vicki, & Rubenstein, Grace. (2015). *Beyond Measure. Rescing an Overscheduled, Overtested, Underestimated Generation.* New York: Simon & Schuster.

American Association for the Advancement of Science (AAAS). (1993). *Benchmarks for science literacy.* New York: Oxford University Press.

American Association for the Advancement of Science (AAAS). (2001). *Atlas of Science Literacy. Project 2061.* Washington, DC: National Science Teachers Association.

American Educational Research Association (AERA), American Psychological Association (APA), & National Council on Measurement in Education (NCME). (2014). *Standards for Education and Psychological Testing.* Washington, DC: AERA.

Andrade, Heidi L., & Cizek, Gregory J. (Eds.). (2010). *Handbook of Formative Assessment.* New York and London: Routledge.

Bennett, Randy Elliot. (2011). Formative assessment: a critical review. *Assessment in Education: Principles, Policy & Practice, 18*(1), 5-25.

Benson, Jeri. (2003). *Editorial. Educational Measurement: Issues and Practice, 22*(4), 4.

Berger, Ron. (2003). *An Ethic of Excellence. Building a Culture of Craftsmanship with Students.* Portsmouth, NH: Heinemann.

Black, Paul, Harrison, Christine, Lee, Clare, Marshall, Bethan, & Wiliam, Dylan. (2004). Working "Inside the Black Box": Assessment for Learning in the Classroom. *Phi Delta Kappan, 86*(1), 8-21.

Bloom, Benjamin S., Engelhart, Max D., Furst, Edward J., Hill, Walker H., & Krathwohl, David R. (Eds.). (1956). Taxonomy of educational objectives: Handbook I: Cognitive domain. New York: David McKay.

Brennan, Robert L. (Ed.). (2006). *Educational Measurement.* Westport, Connecticut: American Council on Education and Praeger Publishers.

Brookhart, Susan M. (2003). Developing Measurement Theory for Classroom Assessment: Purposes and Uses. *Educational Measurement: Issues & Practices*(Winter), 5-12.

Brookhart, Susan M. (2016). *How to Make Decisions with Different Kinds of Student Assessment Data.* Alexandria, VA: ASCD.

Brown, Peter C., Roediger III, Henry L., & McDaniel, Mark A. (2014). *Make it Stick. The Science of Successful Learning.* Cambridge, Massachusetts: The Belknap Press of Harvard University Press.

Carver, Ronald P. (1974). Two Dimensions of Tests: Psychometric and Edumetric. *American Psychologist,* 512-518.

Cizek, Gregory J. (2010). An Introduction to Formative Assessment: History, Characteristics, and Challenges. In H. L. Andrade & G. J. Cizek (Eds.), *Handbook of Formative Assessment.* New York and London: Routledge.

Coburn, Cynthia E., & Penuel, William R. (2016). Research-Practice Partnerships in Education: Outcomes, Dynamics and Open Questions. *Educational Researcher, 45*(1), 48-54.

Cook, Thomas D., Scriven, Michael, Coryn, Chris L. S., & Evergreen, Stephanie D. H. (2010). Contemporary Thinking about Causation in Evaluation: A Dialogue with Tom Cook and Michael Scriven. *American Journal of Evaluation, 31*(1), 105-117.

David, Jane L., & Cuban, Larry. (2010). *Cutting through the Hype. The Essential Guide to School Reform.* Cambridge, Massachusetts: Harvard Education Press.

Deleuze, Gilles, & Guattari, Félix. (1994). *What is Philosophy?* New York: Columbia University Press.

Dewey, John. (1902). *The Child and the Curriculum.* Chicago: The University of Chicago Press.

Dewey, John. (1938). *Experience and Education.* New York: The MacMillan Company.

Doane, William E. J., Rice, Rebekah R., & Zachos, Paul. (2006). Knowing When You Don't Know: Supporting teaching and learning using a new generation of tests. *The Science Teacher, 73*(4).

Doane, William E. J., & Stefl-Mabry, Joette. (2009). Aligning Planning, Instruction, and Assessment in a University Problem-Based Learning, Trans-Generational Web Development Learning Experience. In O.-S. Tan (Ed.), *Problem-based Learning and Creativity:* Thompson Learning.

Dosse, François (2010). *Gilles Deleuze and Félix Guattari: Intersecting Lives* Columbia University Press.

Duckworth, Angela L., & Yeager, David Scott. (2015). Measurement Matters: Assessing Personal Qualities Other Than Cognitive Ability for *Educational Purposes. Educational Researcher, 44*(4), 237-251.

Edwards, Betty. (1989). *Drawing on the Right Side of the Brain: A Course in Enhancing Creativity and Artistic Confidence, Revised Edition.* Los Angeles: Jermy P. Tarcher, Inc.

Feynman, Richard P. (1965). *The Character of Natural Law.* Cambridge, MA: The MIT Press.

Ginsburg, Iona H. (1982). Jean Piaget and Rudolf Steiner: Stages of child development and implications for pedagogy. *Teachers College Record, 84*(2), 327-337.

Gipps, Caroline V. (1999). Socio-cultural aspects of assessment. *Review of Research in Education, 24*(1), 355-392.

Gladstone, Francis. (1997). *Republican Academies. Rudolph Steiner on self-management, experiential study and self-education in the life of a college of teachers.* Sussex, England: Steiner Schools Fellowship.

Glass, Gene V. (2008). *Fertilizers, Pills, and Magnetic Strips: the Fate of Public Education in America.* Charlotte, North Carolina: Information Age Publishing, Inc.

Glass, Gene V., McGaw, Barry, & Smith, Mary Lee. (1981). *Meta-analysis in Social Research.* Beverly Hills, CA: Sage.

Gleick, James. (2011). *The Information. A History. A Theory. A Flood.* New York: Pantheon Books, a division of Random House.

Hattie, John. (2009). *Visible Learning. A synthesis of over 800 meta-analyses relating to achievement.* New York, NY: Routledge. Taylor and Francis Group.

Hattie, John. (2012). *Visible Learning for Teachers.* London and New York: Routledge.

Heritage, Margaret. (2008). Learning Progressions: Supporting Instruction and Formative Assessment.

Hoffman, Banesh. (1962). *The Tyranny of Testing.* U.S.A.: The Crowell-Collier Publishing Company.

Inhelder, Bärbel, & Piaget, Jean. (1958). *The Growth of Logical Thinking. From Childhood to Adolescence.* (A. Parsons & S. Milgram, Trans.). New York: Basic Books, Inc.

Johnson, Mauritz. (1967). Definitions and Models in Curriculum Theory. *Educational Theory, 17,* 127-140.

Johnson, Mauritz. (1977). *Intentionality in Education.* Albany, NY: Center for Curriculum Research and Services, State University of New York at Albany.

Johnson, Mauritz. (1985). Curriculum's Missing Data Base. *Curriculum Inquiry, 15*(4), 359-360.

Johnston, Peter H. (2004). *Choice Words: How Our Language Affects Children's Learning*. Portland, Maine: Stenhous Publishers.

Joint Committee on Standards for Educational Evaluation. (2015). *The Classroom Assessment Standards for PreK-12 Teachers:* Kindle Direct Press.

Kane, Michael T. (2006). Validation. In R. L. Brennan (Ed.), *Educational Measurement.* Westport, Connecticut: American Council on Education and Praeger Publishers.

Kendall, John. (2011). *Understanding Common Core State Standards*. Alexandria, Virginia: ASCD.

Klees, Steven J. (2016). VAMs Are Never "Accurate, Reliable, and Valid". *Educational Researcher, 45*.

Kohn, Alfie. (2000). *The Case Against Standardized Testing*. Portsmouth, NH: Heinemann.

Koretz, Daniel. (2008). Measuring Up. *What Educational Testing Really Tells Us.* Cambridge, Massachusetts: Harvard University Press.

Lampert, Magdalene. (2001). *Teaching Problems and the Problems of Teaching*. New Haven, CT: Yale University Press.

Markham, Thomas. (2011). Project Based *Learning. Teacher Librarian, 39*(2), 38-42.

McDaniel, Mark A., Agarwal, Pooja K., Huelser, Barbie J., McDermott, Kathleen B., & Roediger III, Henry L. (2011). Test-enhanced learning in a middle school science classroom: The effects of quiz frequency and placement. *Journal of Educational Psychology, 103,* 399-414.

McGrayne, Sharon Bertsch. (2011). *The Theory that Would Not Die. How Bayes' rule cracked the enigma code, hunted down Russian submarines, & emerged triumphant from two centuries of controversy.* New Haven & London: Yale University Press.

McMillan, James H. (Ed.). (2013). *Handbook of Research on Classroom Assessment*. Los Angeles: SAGE.

Mislevy, Robert J. (1993). Introduction. In N. Frederiksen, R. J. Mislevy & I. J. Bejar (Eds.), *Test Theory for a New Generation of Tests*. Hillsdale, New Jersey: Lawrence Erlbaum Associates.

Moss, Pamela A. (2003). Reconceptualizing Validity for Classroom Assessment and Grading. *Educational Measurement: Issues and Practice, 22*(4), 13-25.

National Research Council of the National Academies. (2011). *Successful K-12 STEM Education: Identifying Effective Approaches in Science, Technology, Engineering, and Mathematics.* Washington, DC: National Academies Press.

National Research Council of the National Academies. (2013). *Monitoring Progress Toward Successful K-12 STEM Education: A Nation Advancing?* Washington, DC: National Academies Press.

Nichols, Sharon L., & Berliner, David C. (2007). *Collateral Damage: How High-Stakes Testing Corrupts America's Schools.* Cambridge, Massachusetts: Harvard Education Press.

Pellegrino, James W. (2014). A Learning Sciences Perspective on the Design and Use of Assessment in Education. In R. K. Sawyer (Ed.), *The Cambridge Handbook of the Learning Sciences.* New York, NY: Cambridge University Press.

Perrenoud, Philippe. (1998). From formative evaluation to a controlled regulation of learning processes. Towards a wider conceptual field. *Assessment in Education: Principles, Policy and Practice, 5*(1), 85 —102.

Phillips, Lawrence D. (1973). *Bayesian Statistics for Social Scientists:* Nelson.

Piaget, Jean, & Inhelder, Bärbel. (1969). *The psychology of the child.* New York: Basic Books.

Popham, W. James. (1999). Where Large Scale Educational Assessment Is Heading and Why It Shouldn't. *Educational Measurement: Issues And Practice., 18*(3), 13-17.

Popham, W. James. (2011). *Transformative Assessment in Action.* Alexandria, VA: ASCD.

Ravitch, Diane. (1995). *National Standards in American Education. A citizen's guide.* Washington, D.C.: The Brookings Institution.

Ravitch, Diane. (2010). *The Death and Life of the Great American School System. How Testing and Choice are Undermining Education.* New York: Basic Books.

Roediger III, Henry L., Agarwal, Pooja K., McDaniel, Mark A., & McDermott, Kathleen B. (2011). Test-enhanced lerning in the classroom: Long-term improvemens from quizzing. *Journal of Experimental Psychology: Applied, 17*(4), 382-395.

Ruiz-Primo, Maria Araceli. (2004). *Examining Concept Maps as an Assessment Tool.* Paper presented at the First International Conference on Concept Mapping, Pamplona Spain.

Sadler, D. Royce. (1989). Formative assessment and the design of instructional systems. *Instructional Science, 18*(2), 119-144.

Sahlberg, Pasi. (2011). *Finnish Lessons. What can the world learn from educational change in Finland?* New York, NY: Teachers College Press.

Schneider, Rebecca M., & Plasman, Kellie. (2011). Science Teacher Learning Progressions: A Review of Science Teachers' Pedagogical Content Knowledge Development. *Review of Educational Research, 81*(4), 530-565.

Scriven, Michael S. (1967). *The Methodology of Evaluation.* Chicago: Rand McNally.

Shepard, Lorrie A. (2000). The role of assessment in a learning culture. *Educational Researcher, 29*(7), 4-14.

Shute, Valerie J., Leighton, Jacqueline P., Jang, Eunice E., & Chu, Man-Wai. (2016). Advances in the Science of Assessment. *Educational Assessment, 21*(1), 34-59.

Smith, Jeffrey K. (2003). Reconsidering Reliability in Classroom Assessment and Grading. *Educational Measurement: Issues and Practice, 22*(4), 26-33.

Sobel, Dava, & Andrewes, William J. H. (1998). *The Illustrated Longitude. The True Story of a Lone Genius Who Solved the Greatest Scientific Problem of His Time.* New York: Walker and Company.

Stefl-Mabry, Joette, & Doane, William E. J. (2008). *Teaching & Learning 2.0: An urgent call to do away with the isolationist practice of education and retool education as community in the United States.* Paper presented at the Society for Information Technology and Teacher Education (SITE), Las Vegas, Nevada.

Stefl-Mabry, Joette, & Doane, William E. J. (2014). *Teaching to Assess: Lessons Learned When Faculty and Preservice Educators Learn to Assess and Assess to Learn.* Paper presented at the American Educational Research Association Annual Conference, Philadelphia, Pennsylvania.

Tomlinson, Carol Ann. (2002). Invitations to Learn. *Educational Leadership, 60*(1), 6-10.

Tukey, John W. (1969). Analyzing Data: Sanctification or detective work. *American Psychologist, 24,* 83-91.

Vatterott, Cathy. (2015). *Rethinking Grading. Meaningful Assessment for Standards-Based Learning.* Alexandria, VA: ASCD.

Yeh, Stuart S. (2006). *Raising Student Achievement through Rapid Assessment and Test Reform.* New York: Teachers College Press.

Zachos, Paul, Hick, Thomas L., Doane, William E. J., & Sargent, Cynthia. (2000). Setting Theoretical and Empirical Foundations for Assessing Scientific Inquiry and Discovery in Educational Programs. *The Journal of Research in Science Teaching, 37*(9), 938-962.

Index of Names Cited in *Knowing The Learner*

A

Abeles, V. – 88, 153

Agarwal, P.K. – 156, 157

Andrade, H. – 99, 153, 154

Andrewes, W.J.H. – 82, 158

Archimedes – 32

B

Bennett, R.E. – 101, 153

Benson, J. – 78, 153

Berger, R. – 10, 153

Berliner, D.C. – 84, 157

Black, P. – 100, 153

Bloom, B.S. – 21, 82, 153

Brahe, T. – 54

Brennan, R.L. – 79, 153, 156

Brookhart, S.M. – 89, 100, 153

Brown, P. – 21, 89, 90, 121, 154

C

Carlyle, T. – 22

Carver, R.P. – 78, 154

Chu, M-W. – 21, 158

Cizek, G.J. – 99, 101, 153, 154

Coburn, C. – 116, 154

Cook, T.D. – 87, 154

Coryn, C.L.S. – 87, 154

Cuban, L. – 83, 84, 154

D

David, J.L. – 83, 84, 154

Delano, J.W. – 45, 140, 144

Deming, W.E. – 50

Deleuze, G. – 21, 154

Dewey, J. – 16, 26, 82, 154

Doane, W.E.J. – 22, 78, 113, 154, 158

Dosse, F. – 21, 154

Duckworth, A.L. – 22, 154

E

Edwards, B. – 19, 50, 155

Engelhart, M.D. – 21, 153

Evergreen, S.D.H. – 87, 154

F

Feynman, R.P. – 54, 155

Furst, E.J. – 21, 153

G

Ginsburg, I.H. – 26, 155

Gipps, C.V. – 54, 155

Gladstone, F. – 116, 155

Glass, G.V. – 83, 105, 155

Gleick, J. – 18, 155

Guattari, F. – 21, 154

H

Harrison, C. – 82, 100, 153

Hattie, J. – 105, 115, 155

Heritage, M. – 57, 127, 155

Hick, T.L. – 22, 121, 158

Hill, W. H. – 21, 153

Hoffman, B. – 88, 155

Huelser, B.J. – 156

I

Inhelder, B. – viii, 22, 26, 82, 155, 157

J

Jang, E.E. – 21, 158

Johnson, M. – 16, 17, 18, 19, 21, 23, 24, 26, 28, 32, 50, 57, 82, 96, 98, 103, 127, 150, 151, 155

Johnston, P.H. – 6, 7, 156

K

Kane, M.T. – 56, 156

Kendall, J. – 85, 156

Kepler, J. – 54

Khan, S. – 6

Klees, S.J. – 87, 156

Kohn, A. – 88, 90, 156

Koretz, D. – 59, 89, 156

Krathwohl, D.R. – 21, 153

Author Biographies

Dr. Paul Zachos has been teaching in primary schools, secondary schools, and university settings since the 1970s. He has served as researcher, evaluator, and planner for the New York State Education Department. Dr. Zachos has carried out evaluations of educational programs in public and independent schools and in projects funded by the National Science Foundation and NASA. He has a special interest in scientific and educational creativity. He currently offers practical, interactive, online courses in the fundamentals of educational assessment and evaluation. Dr. Zachos holds a PhD in educational psychology and statistics and an MS in curriculum and instruction from the State University of New York at Albany. He holds a BA in comparative language from Queens College of the City University of New York.

Dr. William E. J. Doane has expertise in computer science, computer science education, computer science education research, information science, instructional design, and curriculum development. Before joining IDA's Science and Technology Policy Institute, Dr. Doane was a research associate at the University at Albany and the Association for the Cooperative Advancement of Science & Education. He has taught at the University at Albany, Bennington College, the College of Saint Rose, Skidmore College, and other institutions. Dr. Doane holds a PhD in informatics from the State University of New York at Albany, an MS in information and computer sciences from the University of Hawai'i — Mānoa, and a BA in cognitive science from Hampshire College.

Readers interested in communicating with the authors or engaging in conversation concerning topics presented in Knowing the Learner can do so by visiting the Forum for Educational Arts and Sciences at *http://EducationalRenewal.org/forum/* and clicking on *Knowing the Learner*

CPSIA information can be obtained
at www.ICGtesting.com
Printed in the USA
FSOW04n0404100817
37283FS